THE-CUTTING-EDGE
CLERGY-CAUCUS
PRESENTS:

THEO-BIBLICAL
REFLECTIONS-ON
IMPORTANT-ISSUES
FROM-THE-MARGINS

BLACK LIVES MATTER, INCARCERATION & RESISTANCE TO EMPIRE

FOREWORD
REV. TRENTON LAMAR GREEN

AUTHORS:
RAMONE R. BILLINGSLEY, M.DIV., M.A
KURT S. CLARK, D.MIN.
TYREE A. ANDERSON, D.MIN.

ISBN:
978-0-578-59408-8

COPYRIGHT © 2019

COVER DESIGN BY TYREE A. ANDERSON, D.MIN.

ALL RIGHTS RESERVED. NO PARTS OF THIS BOOK MAY BE REPRODUCED OR TRANSMITTED IN ANY FORM OR BY ANY MEANS, ELECTRONIC OR MECHANICAL, INCLUDING PHOTOCOPYING AND RECORDING, OR BY ANY INFORMATION STORAGE AND RETRIEVAL SYSTEM WITHOUT PERSON IN WRITING FROM THE PUBLISHERS/AUTHORS

CONTENTS

REV. TRENTON LAMAR GREEN
FORWARD FOREWORD... 4

RAMONE R. BILLINGSLEY, M.DIV., M.A.
*A BLACK LIVES MATTER HERMENUTIC:
EXEGETICAL FOUNDATIONS FOR READING AND PREACHING
PROPHETICALLY* 6

KURT S. CLARK, D.MIN.
THE AFRICAN AMERICAN CHURCH: A WORKING DEFINITION 43

TYREE A. ANDERSON, D.MIN.
*A THEO-BIBLICAL CONTEXT FOR CONFRONTING THE ISSUES OF
MARGINALIZATION ENDURED BY THE INCARCERATED* 74

A FORWARD FOREWORD

Rev. Trenton Green

This past summer I was privileged to travel to Cairo, Egypt. I intentionally scheduled my trip during the season of fasting, service, and prayer called Ramadan so that I would be available to tour the city and experience the culture as much as possible. I remember walking through downtown Cairo with my group to find fallen buildings everywhere. After counting about 10 buildings that had fallen and seeing dozens of demolition teams trying to manage and discard the debris, I finally asked the reason.

Our tour guide gave several reasons in response. She said first, most of the buildings are extremely old and have not been occupied for years. And after years of neglect they sometime just cave in. She said in most cases, however, many of these buildings fall because of weak foundations. She said, the foundations of these buildings were built to support three- or four-story buildings. But when families moved in to occupy a floor, if the family has a son it is not uncommon for the son to add another floor onto the building when he gets married to house his new family. So, what you find most times, are buildings with six or seven stories or floors with foundations that were built to hold and support two or three stories. When floors are added but the foundations aren't renovated a fall or collapse of the entire building is inevitable.

Reading the work of Dr. Clark, Dr. Billingsley, and Dr. Anderson, I believe, reveals a need to renovate our "foundations". At the time of this writing we are seeing the topics of this work converge in provocative, even problematic ways. It's been a week since the sentencing of Amber Guyger. It's been a week since we saw the "hug" between Brandt Jean, the brother of slain Botham

Jean, and Amber Guyger, the murderer. It's been a week since Judge Tammy Kemp hugged and handed a bible to Amber Guyger. The critical questions of the "Christian" community have been, what does the Bible say? What must the response of the church be? Was her sentencing fair?

I'm thankful that this work allows and shows the validity of an alternative perspective. It encourages the reader to not be conformed to the mind set and or disposition of state-sanctioned religion. It offers an alternative look at the biblical text. We see a God who liberates His children from imprisoning conditions and incarcerating dispositions. This work offers one the opportunity, as Paul says, to be transformed by the renewing or "renovating of our minds. (Romans 12:2)

Rev. Trenton Green
Besson Divinity School, Senior Master of Divinity Student
Samford University
Birmingham, AL

A BLACK LIVES MATTER HERMENUTIC:
EXEGETICAL FOUNDATIONS FOR READING AND PREACHING PROPHETICALLY

Rev. Ramone R. Billingsley, MDiv., MA

The purpose of this essay is to address the need for Black clergy to read the Bible from the social location of black lives in order for scripture to be relevant in restoring and healing the socio-political and spiritual trauma in the black experience(s). The biblical foundations for this exploration are rooted in two important texts, which are Isaiah 58:1-14 and Luke 4:16-30. The Isaiah text is important because it describes the results of a faith community that chooses to focus on personal worship while ignoring social injustices. It demonstrates the need for the Black Baptist preacher to read, interpret and apply Scripture out of the concerns for Black people. The Lukan passage provides the model, approach and content for the Black preacher as a prophetic voice. Both texts will encourage the Black preacher to develop a hermeneutic for preaching so that the daily struggles of Black life and the local community are not overlooked, but deeply integrated into the way one reads and applies Scripture.

The Black Baptist preaching climate remains deeply entrenched in Eurocentric approaches to reading Scripture and preaching. These approaches focus solely on personal piety to the exclusion of social prophetic engagement. This has stifled the Black Baptist church and stripped away its prophetic vision. Consequently, it creates conditions in which the Black Baptist preacher becomes and remains complicit in the oppression of those to whom she or he preaches.

Some Black Baptist preachers are unable to read Scripture from their own social location because they have been co-opted by white approaches to reading the Bible. Too much emphasis is placed on expository preaching, as done in some white evangelical circles, and discovering the authorial intention of biblical texts.

Although this is a valid approach to reading scripture, it disallows the black preacher opportunities to bring her or his social awareness to the interpretive process. The situation is dire. An emphasis on personal piety and right relationship with God becomes the focus without any social consciousness at the local and state levels. Consequently, the Black Baptist preacher's preaching remains irrelevant by not giving voice to their daily struggles and equipping them with the tools necessary for a communal theopraxis of social engagement.

Isaiah 58:1-14 describes the failed covenantal-relationship within a faith community, who has adopted a worldview and epistemology foreign to the character of its God. Specifically, it runs counter to God's covenantal values for the community. This epistemology is a narrative that has redefined the community's religious values and ethics, so that religious ritual and social justice become each other's enemy. More specifically, it is the result of an emphasis on personal piety to the exclusion of social responsibility. This epistemology forced Israel to forget its heritage as an enslaved people, who had no communal identity, who were nomads without land ownership, who were living at the mercy of a tyrannical king energized by fear and racism, who were constantly crying out to God for justice.

It is a poetic-passionate account of how members of a community opted to adopt a religious narrative and religious practice that allowed one group to benefit from the oppression of another group. It shows how a faith community redefined fasting and sabbath, two of Israel's most sacred ritualistic practices, in a way which willfully excluded and kept "the other" within the community oppressed. This community reordered the moral compass of its religious heritage so as to make social injustice normative and social equality wrong through a reinterpretation of religion through the reinterpretation of rituals. In sum, the dominant group in this Judean community used religion and religious practices to oppress a minority group as the whole community struggled with finding its identity and purpose in relation to God.

Luke 4:16-21 functions as the New Testament foundation for this project. Its significance centers on Jesus' inaugural sermon. Jesus preached this sermon in the temple, which is a geo-political space where politics, religion and justice collide. His sermon content outlines his mission and purpose both as a man, a prophet and public thinker within Luke's Gospel. The sermon is not popular for the establishment because it exposes the oppressors as unjustly profiting off of the oppressed. It bankrupts systems which are designed to make money off people who are sick and socially vulnerable. While exposing this behavior, the sermon lifts up the ideals of justice and righteousness as found in both the Sinai Covenant as well as in Third Isaiah. In fact, Jesus takes this passage from Isaiah 61 and gives it new life, while showing the disciples and the oppressors how to live in right relationship with God, by destroying unjust systems and restoring human relationships.

Jesus' sermon becomes the new norm because it highlights a theopraxis rooted in the Hebrew Bible's concept of justice and righteousness. Normative behavior of injustice is challenged and exposed as antithetical to the core of God's teachings. Jesus' sermon becomes a model for the content and application of A Black Lives Matter Hermeneutic. In a new context, it seeks to liberate biblical interpretation from White Supremacy. It shapes preaching as pastoral which includes both prophetic and priestly while focusing on preaching in action through praxis. It emphasizes good news to the oppressed, the exposure of oppressive systems and a renewed vision of creative ways to engage God from one's storied social location. The concepts of liberation and freedom to worship are at the core.

The remaining parts of this essay will critically analyze Isaiah 58:1-14 and Luke 4:16-30 as the exegetical foundations for a Black Lives Matter Hermeneutic. The critical analysis will begin first with an examination of the historical context highlighting issues of authorship, date and social location. Second, the literary context will be explored. This section will describe the larger and immediate context of the text along with its canonical context. Third, a formal analysis will be explored giving attention to the literary genre of the biblical book, the genre of the focal text as along as the movement of the text. Fourth, 3-4 themes within each passage will be explained. These themes will also be considered within the canonical text of Scripture to determine the relationship between the theme in the focal text and its occurrence in other parts of Scripture. Lastly, a conclusion and summary will be provided to synthesize the material while making foundational connections to the overall project.

OLD TESTAMENT FOUNDATION – ISAIAH 58:1-14[1]

Text

1   Shout out, do not hold back!
        Lift up your voice like a trumpet!
    Announce to my people their rebellion,
        to the house of Jacob their sins.
2   Yet day after day they seek me
        and delight to know my ways,
    as if they were a nation that practiced righteousness
        and did not forsake the ordinance of their God;
    they ask of me righteous judgments,
        they delight to draw near to God.
3   "Why do we fast, but you do not see?
        Why humble ourselves, but you do not notice?"
    Look, you serve your own interest on your fast day,
        and oppress all your workers.

---

[1] Both the Old & New Testament passage listed are taken from the New Revised Standard Version. However, my observations and critical analysis of both passages are based on my own translations and work in the original languages (for the Hebrew text I use BHS 5th Edition and for the Greek text NA28th Edition).

4 Look, you fast only to quarrel and to fight
    and to strike with a wicked fist.
Such fasting as you do today
    will not make your voice heard on high.
5 Is such the fast that I choose,
    a day to humble oneself?
Is it to bow down the head like a bulrush,
    and to lie in sackcloth and ashes?
Will you call this a fast,
    a day acceptable to the LORD?

6 Is not this the fast that I choose:
    to loose the bonds of injustice,
    to undo the thongs of the yoke,
to let the oppressed go free,
    and to break every yoke?
7 Is it not to share your bread with the hungry,
    and bring the homeless poor into your house;
when you see the naked, to cover them,
    and not to hide yourself from your own kin?
8 Then your light shall break forth like the dawn,
    and your healing shall spring up quickly;
your vindicator shall go before you,
    the glory of the LORD shall be your rear guard.
9 Then you shall call, and the LORD will answer;
    you shall cry for help, and he will say, Here I am.

If you remove the yoke from among you,
    the pointing of the finger, the speaking of evil,
10 if you offer your food to the hungry
    and satisfy the needs of the afflicted,
then your light shall rise in the darkness
    and your gloom be like the noonday.
11 The LORD will guide you continually,
    and satisfy your needs in parched places,
    and make your bones strong;
and you shall be like a watered garden,
    like a spring of water,
    whose waters never fail.
12 Your ancient ruins shall be rebuilt;
    you shall raise up the foundations of many generations;
you shall be called the repairer of the breach,
    the restorer of streets to live in.

13 If you refrain from trampling the sabbath,
    from pursuing your own interests on my holy day;

> if you call the sabbath a delight
>> and the holy day of the LORD honorable;
> if you honor it, not going your own ways,
>> serving your own interests, or pursuing your own affairs;
>
> 14 then you shall take delight in the LORD,
>> and I will make you ride upon the heights of the earth;
> I will feed you with the heritage of your ancestor Jacob,
>> for the mouth of the LORD has spoken.

Historical Context

Scholars have debated for decades about the exact date and historical context of Third Isaiah. Also, scholars are unable to determine who wrote Third Isaiah.[2] Several factors complicate the debate regarding the sections. First, this part of Isaiah does not mention any specific historical events, unlike other prophetic texts such as First or Second Isaiah. Similarly, there are no date formulae associated with specific kings (i.e., Isaiah 1:1; Jeremiah 1:1-2; Haggai 1:1). These problems make dating Third Isaiah difficult.[3]

However, there are other inductive clues within this passage which will suggests some possibilities for dating. Some of the clues includes the lack of a wall to protect the community (60:10). The most troubling part is that foreigners are expected to build it. Also, Jerusalem—the capital city and YHWH's home— is lying in ruins. This suggests there is no existing temple in

---

[2] Elizabeth Achtemeier, *The Community and Message of Isaiah 56-66: A Theological Commentary* (Minneapolis: Augsburg Publishing House, 1982), 11.

[3] These factors mentioned are part of general scholarly knowledge about Third Isaiah as found in, the commentaries such as: Joseph Blenkinsop, *Isaiah 56-66: A New Translation with Introduction and Commentary*, Anchor Bible, vol. 19B (New York: Doubleday, 2003) p. 42.

which to worship (61:4; 63:18; 64:9-12). If there is no temple, if the holy city, Jerusalem, is in ruins, then YHWH has no home.[4]

Equally, other important inductive clues focus on religious life. Religious practices during this period were far from the ideals and principles of the worship of YHWH as found in Exodus, Leviticus and particularly Deuteronomy. Instead of an emphasis on Yahwism, religious practices during this period were eclectic. Religious unity and conservatism were exchanged for religious pluralism. This is notable in the prophet's judgment with respect to idolatry (57:3-13; 66:17).

Although there is no general consensus about the date of Third Isaiah, the inductive evidence points to a date around the late sixth century to early fifth century. Also, it is safe to assume that the prophet Isaiah did not write the entire book, since the book covers such a large time period—from the eight to the sixth centuries or early fifth century.[5] As Elizabeth Achtemeier argues, Isaiah 56-66 and therefore Isaiah 40-55, were written by a school or prophetic thinkers associated with the historical Isaiah, who were called "The Isaianic School."[6]

Literary Context

Isaianic scholars do not agree on how the book of Isaiah should be divided. Some scholars argue for a two-fold division consisting of First Isaiah (1-39) and Second Isaiah (40-66). Other scholars, however, argue for a three-fold division consisting of First Isaiah (1-39), Second Isaiah

---

[4] In the ancient world, the capital city and the temple were the place where the nation's deity resided. In Ancient Israel, this was Jerusalem and its temple: Philip P. Jenson, "Temple" in *The Dictionary of the Old Testament Prophets*, ed. Mark J. Boda and J. Gordon McConville (Downers Grove, IL: InterVarsity Press, 2012), 767.

[5] Michael D. Coogan, *The Old Testament: A Historical and Literary Introduction to the Hebrew Bible* (Oxford: Oxford University Press, 2011), 405; Elizabeth Achtemeier, "*The Community and Message of Isaiah 56-66: A Theological Commentary* (Minneapolis: Augsburg Publishing House, 1982), 11.

[6] Elizabeth Achtemeier, *The Community and Message of Isaiah 56-66*, 15.

or Deutero-Isaiah (40-55) and Third Isaiah or Trito-Isaiah (56-66). Each division contains a distinct theology, style, vocabulary and historical context. For the purpose of this paper, I adopt the theory that Isaiah consists of three distinct sections as shown in the following outline:

Outline of The Book of Isaiah[7]

    I.   Judgment and Promise: First Isaiah (1-39)

        a. Oracles against Judah (1-12)

        b. Oracles to foreign nations (13-23)

        c. Yahweh's purpose in future judgment (24-27)

        d. Value of trusting YHWH (28-35)

        e. Historical Interlude (36-39)

    II.   YHWH'S Comfort and Salvation: Second Isaiah (40-55)

        a. Deliverance for the remnant (40-48)

        b. YHWH and reconciliation (49-55)

    III.   Divine Character: Third Isaiah (56-66)

        a. Human inability (56-59)

        b. Glory of Zion (60-62)

        c. Divine ability (63-66)

---

[7] The following commentaries were consulted to produce this outline of Isaiah: Joseph Blenkinsopp, *Isaiah 40-55*. The Anchor Bible (New York: Doubleday, 2002), 59-61; John N. Oswalt, *Isaiah*, The NIV Application Commentary (Grand Rapids: Zondervan, 2003), 65-66; William Sanford LaSor, David Allen Hubbard and Frederic William Bush, *Old Testament Survey: The Message, Form, and Background of the Old Testament*, 2nd edition (Grand Rapids: Eerdmans), 290-292.

Each of the above sections has its own unique theology, theme and style. For instance, First Isaiah emphasizes themes of judgment for both Israel and foreign nations, calls to repentance, restoration and eschatology. Second Isaiah emphasizes themes of restoration for post-exilic Israel. Third Isaiah emphasizes themes of social justice and religious practice, rebuilding the temple, expanding the community to include those previously excluded such as foreigners and eunuchs, along with a vision of a new heaven and new earth.[8] The prophet arranges these eleven chapters (56-66) in a chiastic structure. Significantly, chapter 61 forms the center of this chiastic structure.[9] This chapter describes a message of liberation and the execution of justice for the oppressed. The Gospel of Luke incorporates the Septuagint version of this text in Luke 4 to describe the prophetic ministry and mission of Jesus. In light of the canonical context, however, Isaiah's message proclaims a universal theme of redemption which are inclusive of Israel and all nations at-large. YHWH's redemptive concerns are for the well-being of all people regardless of their ethnicity, gender or nationhood.

Isaiah 58 is situated in the larger context of Third Isaiah (56-66). The theological focus of this section is rebuilding the community and the struggle to find identity s God's people during postexilic times.[10] This is in contrast to Second Isaiah, which focuses on encouraging and bringing comfort to those who are in exile. Second Isaiah does this by using traditions such as the Exodus, the Abrahamic traditions, etc., while

---

[8] Michael D. Coogan, "*The Old Testament*," 423.

[9] J. Severino Croatto, "Isaiah 56-66" in *The Global Bible Commentary*, ed. Daniel Patte (Nashville: Abingdon Press, 2004), 202-203.

[10] Richard J. Clifford, S.J., "Isaiah Book of" in *The New Interpreter's Dictionary of the Bible*, vol. 3 (Nashville: Abingdon Press, 2009), 86.

re-contextualizing them. However, Richard Clifford notes, Third Isaiah focuses on themes such as the holy mountain of God, restoration of the land, and rebuilding the community and maintaining justice.[11] Executing justice and creating a community that no longer excludes people based on race, ethnicity, gender and nationality remains the focal point of God's redemptive plan. Third Isaiah demonstrates God's intentions, blessings and judgment so this can be accomplished.

Third Isaiah situates chapter 58 near the beginning of its prophecy. Although chapter 58 focuses on the connection between worship and justice, the prophet addresses other communal issues before attacking Israel's false personal piety. Third Isaiah opens with chapter 56 centering the outcasts within the community. This is significant because the larger Israelite community is already a religious and ethnic minority during this period. However, the prophet his message exhorting the people to maintain justice and righteousness (56:3). God's intention is to rebuild the larger community and he begins by highlighting two groups of people who are further marginalized within the community: foreigners and eunuchs (56:3-4, 6). In fact, the prophet encourages the foreigners to accept that they have been allowed to live in full status within the community (56:3). God no longer makes a separation between the native person and the foreigner in the new community. Also, the eunuch receives favor from God as he keeps the sabbath and remain faithful to the covenant. As a result, God promises him material blessings such as an everlasting name (i.e., heritage) and housing with protection (56:4).

The prophet exposes the leaders and summons the animals of the fields to attack them (56:9-12). The leaders are referred to as "watchmen" (56:10) who are blind, meaning they have no spiritual vision or no ability to discern and carryout God's core values. They are likened to a silent dog without a bark, an insatiable appetite and going their own way by following their instincts

---

[11] Richard J. Clifford, S.J., "Isaiah Book of," 87.

instead of the covenant (56:10-12). In Isaiah 57:14-21, the prophet exhorts the people to make a pathway for God's arrival (57:14), which is reminiscent of Isaiah 40. Also, God extends his grace, restoration and comfort to the righteous (57:14, 18-19). The passage ends with a description of the wicked in comparison to the sea being without peace (57:20-21).

Isaiah's preaching shifts attention to the sabbath, injustice and worship (58:1-14). Israel had focused on practicing rituals and maintaining worship traditions within their community. Although they were focused on personal piety, their neglect of those who were marginalized tainted their worship practices. Here the prophet redefines the ritual of fasting as administering justice to the oppressed.

Formal Analysis

Isaiah's prophecies are a collection of prophecies written in poetry and prose. Most prophecies in this book are written in poetic form while others are penned in the narrative style of the historical books (i.e., Isaiah 37-39). The prophet uses an array of literary genres to communicate his message to the exilic and postexilic communities, including but not limited to: prophetic vision reports (21:1-10); call narrative (6); prophetic pronouncement (13:1); trial speech (41:1-5); woe oracles (5:8-24); and prophetic liturgy (12; 33).[12] Second Isaiah communicates its message using disputation (40:12-17), trial speech (43:22-28), hymn (42:10-13) and an oracle of salvation (41:14-16).[13] Within Third Isaiah, the prophet re-contextualizes standard literary genres

---

[12] Marvin A. Sweeney, *Isaiah 1-39 with an Introduction to Prophetic Literature.* The Forms of The Old Testament Literature vol. 16 (Grand Rapids: Eerdmans, 1996), 15-30.

[13] R.N. Whybray, *The Second Isaiah.* Old Testament Guides (Sheffield: Sheffield Academic Press, 1997), 25-39.

within the prophetic tradition to convey his message.[14] He uses judgement oracles (56:9-12; 57:3-13; 58:1-14), laments (59:1-15a; 63:7—64:12), oracles of salvation (65:8-16) and several others.

As it relates to Isaiah 58:1-14, the literary genre is obviously poetry. This is characteristic of the Hebrew prophets in genre. They often preach their messages of salvation, comfort and judgment through poetry. Some prophets such as Jonah and Amos, however, use both narrative and poetry. Grace Emmerson rightly lists Isaiah 58 under the category of judgment oracle that calls out the sins of the people.[15] It also exhorts them to perform behavior that addresses the injustice of the oppressed and the favor of YHWH. Within in these poetic verses, Isaiah uses Hebrew parallelism along with an inclusio to structure this text. The inclusio centers around the word "Jacob" in v. 1 and 14. In v. 1, the phrase "house of Jacob" is used and in v. 14, the phrase "heritage of Jacob" is used.[16] Poetic literature in the Hebrew Bible uses this structuring device to show the limitation of the text.[17] The verses between the inclusio will deal with one general topic.

He uses a variety of literary genres to convey his message. This gives his message variety and always him to emphasize certain theological themes through shifts in genre. Brevard Childs describes vv. 1-4 as an accusation formula.[18] The prophet uses prophetic exhortation to describe the need to cry out and declare YHWH's message (58:1). The verse will begin with an imperative verb with an exhortative tone. In verse 3, he shifts to the genre of a probing question to encourage

---

[14] Grace I. Emerson, Isaiah 56-66. Old Testament Guides (Sheffield: Sheffield Academic Press, 1992), 20-21.

[15] Grace I. Emmerson, *Isaiah 56-66*, 25.

[16] Paul V. Niskanen, *Isaiah 56-56*. Beriot Olam Studies in Hebrew & Narrative Poetry (Collegeville: MN, 2014), 19.

[17] Wilfred G. E. Watson, *Classical Hebrew Poetry: A Guide to its Techniques* (New York: T&T Clark International, 2005), 284-285.

[18] Brevard Childs, *Isaiah*. The Old Testament Library (Louisville: Westminster John Knox Press, 2001), 476.

Israel's introspection regarding her ritual practice and accompanying attitude. He also does this in order to bring attention to Israel's desire for her own pleasure at the expense of others' well-being (vv. 4). The probing question genre continues in vv. 5-8 in order to highlight the connection between ritual observance of fasting along with their lack of social responsibility. In vv. 9a—13, Isaiah shifts to another genre where he uses if-then or conditional clauses, to intensify the connection between worship and justice.[19] The if-clause begins with some turning one's attention to the condition of the oppressed. The then-clause describes a positive outcome for the nation.

To discuss and conceptualize this passage, these verses can be divided into three major sections. The following division is based on shifts in the passage's tone, language, emphasis and content. The following outline describes the overall outline and shape of this text:

I. Exposing Religious Hypocrisy (vv. 1-4)

II. Personal Piety and Justice (vv. 5-7)

III. Conditions for a Healthy Community (vv. 8-14)

Thematic Analysis

The first theme within this passage concerns exposing religious hypocrisy. The prophet begins this judgment oracle in v. 1 with an exhortation and call to summon the people to consider their transgression. To summon the people's attention, the prophet uses two bicola in synonymous parallelism to emphasize both the exhortation, the means of the exhortation and the general content of the exhortation:

קְרָא בְגָרוֹן אַל־תַּחְשֹׂךְ	Scream with [your] throat! So that you do not hold back!

---

[19] Brevard Childs, *Isaiah*, 476.

כַּשּׁוֹפָר הָרֵם קוֹלֶךָ	Like the ram's horn, raise your voice!

YHWH exhorts the prophet to scream with his throat (קְרָא בְגָרוֹן) emphasizing the urgency of this judgment oracle. Equally, it admonishes the prophet to use every aspect of his vocal apparatus to make sure no one misses this message. The significance here is that not only does this colon begin with the typical qal imperative verb קְרָא but this is the only time in the Hebrew Bible YHWH explicitly commands a prophet to scream with his throat.[20] The second part of v. 1a uses a qal imperfect verb in verbal sequence with the preceding imperative. The qal imperfect verb here expresses the purpose of the preceding action: "Scream with [your] throat so that you do not hold back." The second half of the bicola begins with the simile כַּשּׁוֹפָר (like a ram's horn/shophar) הָרֵם קוֹלֶךָ (raise your voice). The synonymous parallelism intensifies as the prophet is told to raise his voice like a ram's horn. This instrument is often used in the context of Israelite worship or in a military context to announce war.

The second bicola in verse 1 describes the general topic of the prophet's message. In v. 1b the prophet is to explain the community's rebellion. The prophet uses continuity of terms to describe the people and their sin. The phrase "my people" occurs in parallel with "Jacob." The colon moves from a general phrase, my people to a specific term "Jacob," which is a referent to those who trace their lineage back to their ancestor and patriarch Jacob.

YHWH also uses continuity of terms with respect to sin. First, he tells the prophet to declare to my people their rebellion. Then in the next phrase by way of verbal ellipsis, to declare to the

---

[20] The phrase קְרָא בְגָרוֹן (Scream from/with [your] throat] occurs nowhere else in the Hebrew Bible.

house of Jacob their sins. The Hebrew word for rebellion is פֶּשַׁע (*peśaʾ*) which originates in a political context. Some English translations translate this word as "transgression." In political contexts, rebellion is an act of defiance when a conquered subject refuses to follow the agreed upon guidelines from his conqueror. Here in this passage, YHWH's people rebelled against him by refusing to follow certain prescriptions of the Sinai covenant (Exodus 19-24) as originally agreed upon. Rebellion here is characterized as a חַטָּאת (sin) since the term occurs in a word pair. Therefore, the judgment oracle comes as a result of the people of God breaching YHWH's covenant.

The prophet addresses the general issue of the community's hypocrisy in vv. 1-4. Although the judgment oracle is given to the community at-large, it is directed to the upper-class and those who are in power. This is evident in later verses when the prophet challenges the community to address the living conditions of those at the bottom of the social ladder. This faith community prides itself on seeking YHWH, delighting in his ways and drawing near to him (v. 2). The word for seek here is דָּרַשׁ (*dāraś*) means one who looks to YHWH for answers and directions concerning right living. Since this word occurs in the imperfect aspect, it suggests that the action of seeking YHWH is incomplete or underway. But the verb is followed by the word יָדַע (*yādaʾ*) which is an infinitive construct. יָדַע has a range of meanings, but in this context, it means to gain personal knowledge about YHWH and how he functions and behaves as God. However, the prophet questions the faith community's purpose for seeking YHWH.

A second theme in this passage is hypocrisy and a disregard for practicing justice. Although they seek to know YHWH and his ways, they do not practice צְדָקָה (*ṣĕdāqāh*) righteousness and they disregard מִשְׁפָּט (*mišpāṭ*) justice (v. 2). The word-pair צְדָקָה/מִשְׁפָּט (*ṣĕdāqāh/mišpāṭ*) occurs frequently in the Hebrew prophets. In the Book of Isaiah is occurs 26 times and is quite significant.[21] Also whether the community practices justice and righteous relates to if YHWH will enact salvation on the community.[22] This suggests that YHWH works in partnership with humanity to accomplish his purposes. In fact, the word-pair is used in 56:1 to open Third Isaiah which sets the theological tone and emphasis for this section. E.R. Hayes argues that this word-pair binds all three major sections together.[23] Justice here in Isaiah 58, refers to restoring anything taken unjustly from people who are without power, high social status or economically rich.[24] This is what it means to be righteous or in right relationship with God. Care for the widows, orphans, strangers, and those who are economically or socially destitute is part of what it means to maintain YHWH's covenant.

The practice of justice is at the core of what it means to be in relationship to God. In fact, justice is etched into a significant part of YHWH's covenant with ancient Israel. Practicing justice was evidence that the faith community was fulfilling its covenant obligations with YHWH.[25] Executing justice within the community was a way for the community to reflect the character and morality of God. Depriving someone of justice was a way of smearing YHWH's reputation and character. YHWH's covenant is not about an individual responsibility to YHWH, but it is mainly about ways to live in community with others. This is clear in parts of the Holiness code in the Book of Leviticus (Lev. 19:9-18). For example, the theme of care for one's neighbor is root in YHWH's

---

[21] I use Accordance Bible software to perform this statistical data.

[22] John Goldingay, *The Theology of the Book of Isaiah* (Downers Grove: IL, IVP Academic, 2014), 76.

[23] Elizabeth R. Hayes, "Justice, Righteousness" in *The Dictionary of the Old Testament Prophets* ed. Mark J. Boda and J. Gordon McConville (Downers Grove: InterVarsity Press, 2012), 468.

[24] Harold V. Bennett, "Justice, OT" in *The New Interpreter's Dictionary of the Bible.* vol. 3 ed. Katherine Dobb Sakenfeld (Nashville: Abingdon Press, 20), 477.

[25] Brian P. Irwin, "Social Justice," in *The Dictionary of the Old Testament Prophets* ed. Mark J. Boda and J. Gordon McConville (Downers Grove: InterVarsity Press, 2012), 721-722.

covenant stipulations. As farmers harvest their crop and removed grapes from their vineyards, YHWH admonished them to leave something behind for the poor and the stranger (vv. 9-10). Not creating financial difficulties on people by holding their paychecks until the next day was equally forbidden (v. 13).

A third theme in this passage is using religious rituals as a way to avoid practicing justice and ethical behavior. Two religious rituals are mentioned in this text: fasting and sabbath. The concept of fasting will be addressed here while the practice of the sabbath will be addressed in the New Testament portion of this chapter. Fasting is an ancient ritual of mourning where the person who fasts abstains from food.[26] Often times this involves a public sign of humility by wearing sackcloth and ashes. In Isaiah 58, the entire community is fasting but the reasons for the fast are not given. One can assume that this piece of missing information is not important to the text. However, the purpose for this fast is not to seek YHWH (v. 3). The Judean community removed the associated sanctity and theological significance and effects of fasting and replaced it with their own pursuits. The prophet juxtaposes the practice of fasting with the current behavior of the community. Although fasting is a worship ritual, it is null and void of sincerity for the following reasons: physical violence among members in the community (v. 4), focusing on making money and transacting business deals that benefit only the business owners while oppressing the workers (v. 3)[27] However, the prophet connects sincere worship through fasting with the practice of social justice. The prophet calls upon the people to fast through removing bonds and yokes that produce wickedness (v. 6), feeding those who are without food (v. 7), and providing housing arrangements

---

[26] David A. Lambert, "Fast, Fasting" in *The New Interpreter's Dictionary of the Bible*, vol. 2 ed. Katherine Doob Sakenfeld (Nashville: Abingdon Press, 2009), 431.

[27] Shalom Paul, Isaiah 40-66: Translation and Commentary. Eerdmans Critical Commentary, ed. David Noel Freedman (Grand Rapids: Eerdmans Publishing, 2012), 484

for the homeless (v. 7). For YHWH, these just practices allow the community to be the people whom he has created them to be (vv. 8). It also will rebuild the once thriving community into a robust faith community (v. 12, 14). This text is reminiscent of Amos 5:21-24. Similarly, the prophet Amos chastises the northern kingdom for focusing on rituals without providing justice for the socioeconomically depraved. The language, however, is much stronger. Amos speaks YHWH's words against Israel's rituals stating that he hates their feasts, solemn assemblies, offerings and songs (vv. 21-23). Instead, the way to please YHWH is removing societal barriers which prevent justice from reaching everyone in need (v. 24).

NEW TESTAMENT FOUNDATION – LUKE 4:16-21

Text

16 When he came to Nazareth, where he had been brought up, he went to the synagogue on the sabbath day, as was his custom. He stood up to read,

17 and the scroll of the prophet Isaiah was given to him. He unrolled the scroll and found the place where it was written:

18   "The Spirit of the Lord is upon me,
            because he has anointed me
                to bring good news to the poor.
        He has sent me to proclaim release to the captives
            and recovery of sight to the blind,
                to let the oppressed go free,

19   to proclaim the year of the Lord's favor."

20 And he rolled up the scroll, gave it back to the attendant, and sat down. The eyes of all in the synagogue were fixed on him.

21 Then he began to say to them, "Today this scripture has been fulfilled in your hearing."

Historical Context

Scholars have debated the authorship of the Gospel of Luke. Unlike most of the prophetic books in the Hebrew Bible, there is no name attached to the Gospel of Luke. There is no superscription which would include a major historical reference, event or date. This is consistent with all four gospels. None of them contain the name or scribal signatory of its author or composer or its intended audience. As Darrell L. Bock has noted, this situation forces scholars to determine authorship and date through other means.[28]

The scholarly consensus argues that Luke, the physician authored The Gospel of Luke as well as the Book of Acts.[29] Similarly, many see a connection between Acts and Luke and refer to Acts as the sequel to Luke. This essay adopts the argument that Luke the physician authored the Gospel of Luke. This argument, as held by Darrell Bock and others, centers on two key pieces of evidence.[30]

Like Bock, scholars note that the author of Luke's Gospel was not an eyewitness of the events in Jesus' ministry. In fact, Luke 1:1-4 the writer acknowledges his purpose is two-fold: to compile a narrative about things which took place in Jesus' ministry by examining several sources, and to present an orderly account to a person named Theophilus. Second, Luke is identified as having accompanied the apostle Paul during Paul's ministry (Acts 16:10-17; 20:5-15; 21:1-18; 27:1-28:16). In addition, Luke is mentioned as one who traveled with Paul in some of the Pauline

---

[28] Darrell L. Bock, "Luke, Gospel of," in *The Dictionary of Jesus and the Gospels*, ed. Joel B. Green and Scot McKnight (Downers Grove: InterVarsity Press, 1992), 495.

[29] Darrell L. Bock, *The Dictionary of Jesus and the Gospels*, p. 496.

[30] Darrell L. Bock, *Luke Volume 1: 1:1-9:50*. Baker Exegetical Commentary on the New Testament (Grand Rapids: Baker Books, 2002), 4.

letters (Philemon 24; Colossians 4:14). Joel Green in his Luke commentary, however, does not give attention to the issue of Luke-Acts authorship because "…our ability or inability to identify the author of the Third Gospel is unimportant to its interpretation."[31] For some scholars, authorship is an exercise in historical reconstruction which is not always conclusive. Likewise, the date of Luke's Gospel is equally debated. Many scholars, however, date the book after the fall of Jerusalem.[32]

An important historical institution mentioned in this text is the synagogue. They synagogue was an important locale in the Jewish communities. It served both a religious function as well as a civic function in the life of the community.[33] The Greek word for synagogue is συναγωγή which means a gathering, collection or assembly. The synagogue developed during postexilic times, which was a place where rabbis taught the Torah, offered prayers and read Scripture. Other sacred rituals were also performed in the synagogue. Luke portrays Jesus' teaching in the synagogue regularly. As noted by Edwin Yamauchi notes, the synagogue also served the civic needs of the community. For example, people who violated the law were punished (Mark 13:9; John 12:42) and a community treasury was stored there. Also, babies were dedicated in the synagogue. Lastly, Jesus clashed with Jewish leaders in the synagogue as he healed and taught about the kingdom of God (Mark 3:1-6).

---

[31] Joel B. Green, *The Gospel of Luke*. The New International Commentary on the New Testament (Grand Rapids: William B. Eerdmans, 1997), 20.

[32] Darrell L. Bock, "*The Dictionary of Jesus and the Gospels*," 498.

[33] Edwin Yamauchi, "Synagogue," in *The Dictionary of Jesus and the Gospels*, ed. Joel B. Green and Scot McKnight (Downers Grove: InterVarsity Press, 1992), 782.

Literary Context

Luke's Gospel occurs third in the canonical gospels after Mark and before John. Joel Green divides the Gospel into eight sections: Prologue (1:1-4), birth and childhood of Jesus (1:5-2:52), preparation for ministry of Jesus (3:1-4:13), Jesus' ministry in Galilee (4:14-9:50), Jesus prepares for Jerusalem (9:51-19:48), Jesus in temple (20:1-21:38), suffering and death of Jesus (22:1-23:56), and the exaltation of Jesus (24:1-53).[34]

The larger literary context of Luke 4:16-21 occurs within the first part of the gospel which consists of Luke 4:14-9:50. This section describes Jesus' ministry in Galilee, which his hometown. Prior to this section, the Gospel begins with a prologue (1:1-4) which describes why the Gospel was written and to whom it was written. An account of birth of Jesus along with his childhood immediately follows (1:5-2:52). This section highlights events happening prior to Jesus' birth emphasizing John's birth (1:57-80), Mary's encounter with an angel announcing her unexpected pregnancy (1:26-38), Jesus birth in the context of social and political upheaval (2:1-20) and his infant days in the temple (2:21-39). Immediately following Jesus' infancy and childhood, Luke focuses on Jesus' preparation for ministry (3:1-4:13). This section describes his relationship with John the Baptist (3:1-20), and his preparation and consecration in the wilderness (4:1-13).

The immediate context of Luke 4:16-21 occurs in the larger context of 4:14-9:50 and in the immediate segment of 4:14-30. Jesus has been baptized (3:1-20) and then spends time in the wilderness where he is tempted (4:1-13), which proves he is not just the son of God, but an obedient and faithful son. This temptation experience and gave him power to do ministry. It is the prerequisite for his ministry activity, which Luke describes as Jesus empowered by the power of

---

[34] Joel B. Green, *The Gospel of Luke*, 25-29.

the Spirit to teach in the synagogue (4:14-15). This is important because Jesus faces constant opposition from those connected to the synagogue.

The literary placement of Luke 4:14-21 is significant in Luke's Gospel. As previously stated, this text occurs at the beginning of Jesus' teaching, preaching and ministry. However, Luke uses this text to set the agenda of Jesus' mission and the way Jesus functions throughout the gospel. The rhetorical effect and message of this passage shocks those in the temple. Jesus is portrayed as a prophet, a liberator and catalyst to ignite God's new kingdom. Jesus' sermon describes people who are oppressed. Luke's Gospel consistently characterizes Jesus as coming to their aid. Essentially, Jesus comes to provide liberation to the outcasts of various communities.

In the canonical context, Luke 4:14-21 shares a primary theme of liberation other Scripture. For example, Jesus quotes Isaiah 61:1-2 which highlights YHWH's spirit empowering the prophet to bring good news to the oppressed. This is consistent with the character of YHWH in Third Isaiah (56-66). The Isaianic text begins with an exhortation for the people to keep and maintain justice for the oppressed (Isaiah 56:1). This theme occurs throughout Isaiah, as stated in the Hebrew Bible/Old Testament section of this project. A comparison of the Greek language used in both Isaiah 61:1-12 and Luke 4:18-19 shows great similarity.

Isaiah 61:1-2 (LXX)	NA28 Greek NT

1 Πνεῦμα κυρίου ἐπ' ἐμέ, οὗ εἵνεκεν ἔχρισέν με· εὐαγγελίσασθαι πτωχοῖς ἀπέσταλκέν με, ἰάσασθαι τοὺς συντετριμμένους τῇ καρδίᾳ, κηρύξαι αἰχμαλώτοις ἄφεσιν καὶ τυφλοῖς ἀνάβλεψιν,
 	
 2 καλέσαι ἐνιαυτὸν κυρίου δεκτὸν καὶ ἡμέραν ἀνταποδόσεως, παρακαλέσαι πάντας τοὺς πενθοῦντας,
	18 πνεῦμα κυρίου ἐπ' ἐμὲ
	     οὗ εἵνεκεν ἔχρισέν με
	 εὐαγγελίσασθαι πτωχοῖς,
	     ἀπέσταλκέν με,
	 κηρύξαι αἰχμαλώτοις ἄφεσιν
	     καὶ τυφλοῖς ἀνάβλεψιν,
	 ἀποστεῖλαι τεθραυσμένους ἐν ἀφέσει,
	
	 19 κηρύξαι ἐνιαυτὸν κυρίου δεκτόν.

Similarly, Jesus' temple sermon shares this theme of liberation and justice for the oppressed as found in Jeremiah's temple (7:1-20). In Jeremiah's sermon, the people of YHWH are focusing on worship but without any regard to how the community treats its members. There is a disconnect between worship and justice. There Jeremiah preaches judgment against the community while emphasizing a call to pursue justice in interpersonal relationships.

Lastly, Jesus' temple sermon echoes the year of Jubilee in the Hebrew Bible. The Year of Jubilee occurs every seven years (Leviticus 25; Deuteronomy 15;1, 7, 12, 18). The seventh year is a year of liberation—all debts are cancelled, people are to assist liberally with the needs with one's neighbor, slaves who were originally sold to their masters are released and generous provisions are given to the flock. The year of Jubilee is not just for humankind, but for all of creation.[35] Robert Sloan describes the important role of the Jubilee Year in Luke's Gospel. He argues that Luke uses

---

[35] Sharon H. Ringe, "Jubilee, Year of," in *The New Interpreter's Dictionary of the Bible*, vol. 3 ed. Katherine Doob Sakenfeld (Nashville: Abingdon Press, 2009), 418.

the Jubilee year motif to discuss issues of redemption, release and Jesus' eschatological purpose.[36] Also, he rightly argues that this motif is important for understanding Luke's beatitudes, the sabbath, the Lord's prayer and Jesus as the messiah.

Formal Analysis

Generally, the literary genre of the Book of Luke is categorized as a gospel. As scholars note, the Greek text of Luke, however, does not refer to it as a gospel. This was an interpretative addition which occurred later in church history.[37] It is called a gospel because like the three other canonical gospels, it describes actions of Jesus' life and ministry on earth. Scholars liken the gospel genre to a Greek genre known as a *bios*. A *bios* is a literary work in which a known heroic figure is central to the work. It describes selected aspects of the hero's life such as his birth, childhood, and key events in the figure's life. An important point worth noting, is that a *bios* is not intended to be comprehensive, but only select. This helps explain why the four canonical gospels are different in their arrangement of material and their content.

As Luke Timothy Johnson argues, Luke's Gospel functions as a narrative.[38] This is true and helps to address the real purpose of this book's existence without getting stifled with arguments and debates about the gospel genre. First, Luke himself describes his work as a narrative compiled from different sources so as to present an orderly account of events in Jesus' ministry

---

[36] Robert B. Sloan, "Jubilee," in *The Dictionary of Jesus and the Gospels*, ed. Joel B. Green and Scott McKnight (Downers Grove: InterVarsity Press, 1992), 396-397.

[37] Willem S. Vorster, "Gospel Genre," in *Anchor Yale Bible Dictionary* vol. 2, ed. David Noel Freeman (New York: Doubleday, 1992), 1077; David deSilva, *An Introduction to the New Testament: Contexts, Methods & Ministry Formation* (Downers Grove, IL: InterVarsity Press, 2004), 146-147.

[38] Luke Timothy Johnson, The Gospel of Luke. Sacra Pagina Series. vol. 3 (Collegeville, Minnesota: The Liturgical Press, 1991), 3-5.

(1:1-4). This also gives insight into why Luke's Gospel contains stories not present in the other gospels (i.e., parable of rich fool 12:16-21, the good Samaritan 10:30-35, parable of the lost son 15:11-32, among others). Second, Acts is rightly described as a sequel to Luke. Therefore, Luke Timothy Johnson concludes,

> "Luke-Acts must also be read as a single story. Acts not only continues the story of the Gospel but provides Luke's own authoritative commentary on the first volume. Any discussion of Luke's purposes, or the development of his themes, must take into account the entire two-volumes work."[39]

Scholars are divided on the exact genre of Luke 4:16-30. As Darrell Bock observes, the genre debate ranges from a pronouncement story, a rejection narrative or a fulfillment story.[40] For the purpose of this exegesis, I will label this text as a story containing several genre imprints.[41] The basic genre of the text is narrative. Also, the main focus of the text concerns Jesus' rejection from his hometown. The story of Jesus' rejection is told using a pronouncement (v. 21), a speech-sermon (vv. 18-19), a proverb (v. 23) and a controversy (vv. 24-30). Therefore, I will allow the overall thrust to guide how the story is labeled. Darrell Bock provides a helpful six-part outline of the passage which captures its overall shape:

 I. "Setting of the Scripture reading (4:16-17)

 II. Cycle 1: Scripture reading and its exposition (4:18-21)

 III. Cycle 1 response: the initial questioning of the crowd (4:22)

 IV. Cycle 2: a proverb and historical picture of their rejection (4:23-27)

---

[39] Luke Timothy Johnson, *The Gospel of Luke*, 4.

[40] Darrell L. Bock, *Luke 1:1—9:50*, 398.

[41] I use Marvin Sweeney's approach to form criticism as a model to describe the form of Hebrew texts. Marvin Sweeney, "Form Criticism," in *To Each its Own Meaning: An Introduction to Biblical Criticisms and Their Application*. Revised and Expanded, edited by Steven L. McKenzie and Stephen Haynes (Louisville: Westminster John Knox Press, 1999), 75-78.

V.   Cycle 2 response: the crowd's anger and hostile desire (4:28-29)

VI. Jesus' departure (4:30)"[42]

The above outline shows two important features which Joel Green notes concerning the movement of the story. First, the narrative itself is self-contained because it begins and ends with an inclusio of action centered on the Greek verb ἔρχομαι (to come).[43] The narrative begins with Jesus entering or coming into the synagogue (v. 16) and not knowing what to expect. The story ends with Jesus quickly leaving the town to escape the mob. In v. 30, the Greek verb διέρχομαι (to go through, to pass through) is used to describe Jesus passing through the rage-filled crowd.

Second, there is the sequence of address followed by a response. In vv. 16-21 Jesus addresses the crowd with his prophetic words. However, in v. 22 the crowd responds with the emotion of amazement. Then in vv. 23-27, Jesus describes their history of rejecting prophets. Again, in vv. 28-29 the crowd responds with rage-filled emotion accompanied with attempted physical assault (v. 30). This story is filled with action, political tension and varied emotions.

Thematic Analysis

There are several themes in this text which deserve a closer examination. The first theme concerns Jesus' ministry in the synagogue on the sabbath day. In the historical context section of this paper, a short description of nature and function of the synagogue was provided. Again, this was an institution where Jews gathered primarily for worship. The synagogue, however, was the place where Torah was read and interpreted. The English term Torah is the Hebrew word תּוֹרָה

---

[42] Darrell L. Bock, *Luke 1:1—9:50*, 399.

[43] Joel B. Green, *The Gospel of Luke*, 207-208.

which means "instruction or teaching" mostly associated with the YHWH's varied instructions to Israel.[44] The Torah readings sometimes consisted of reading passages from the prophets, which is the case in this text. The gospel writers frequently participating in synagogue worship. Specifically, they portray Jesus preaching and teaching in the synagogue. For instance, Luke further describes Jesus teaching in the synagogue which is sometimes followed by a public action (13:10). In Luke 13:10, this is followed by Jesus healing a woman who had been crippled for eighteen years. Mark's Gospel, likewise, consistently describes Jesus' relationship to the synagogue as one of teaching and preaching.

However, Jesus' presence in the synagogue often stirred controversy with religious leaders. Mark, for example, describes a series of controversies between Jesus and the religious leaders. There was a controversy over Jesus' authority to forgive sins (Mark 2:5-11), his habit of befriending people who are society's outcasts which included tax collectors and sinners (2:16-17), his disciples not keeping fasting protocols like the disciples of John and the Pharisees (2:18-22), his redefinition of the sabbath day and the relationship of ministry to the sabbath (2:23-27), as well as Jesus' practice of healing people on the sabbath day (3:1-6). Luke's Gospel equally picks up the theme of controversy on the sabbath because Jesus healed a crippled woman (Luke 13:10-17). In Luke 4:14-30, Jesus' first synagogue controversy in Luke's Gospel is the result of him declaring liberation to the oppressed. This controversy resulted in attempted aggravated assault against Jesus, in which people chased him out of the town (v. 28-30).

The practice of the sabbath is a common feature in a controversy with Jesus' ministry practice. The Greek word for sabbath is σάββατον (*sabbaton*). In Jewish culture σάββατον refers

---

[44] Lawrence H. Schiffman, "Torah" in *The New Interpreter's Dictionary of the Bible*, vol. 5, ed. Katherine Doob Sakenfeld (Nashville: Abingdon Press, 2009), 629.

to the Hebrew word שַׁבָּת (*ŝabbat*) which means the cessation of work on the seventh day of the week.[45] The theological significance for this is evidenced in the creation story. In Genesis 2:2 God rested on the seventh day from his six-day labor of creating the world. Also, the day was sanctified and blessed because of this (v. 3). When God established his covenant with Israel, he made the seventh day a sabbath to imitate his model of working six days while resting on the seventh (Exodus 19:8-9; Deuteronomy 5:12-15). However, in Deuteronomy, the sabbath was a day not only to rest from working, but also to reflect on YHWH's work of delivering Israel from Egyptian slavery (Deuteronomy 5:14-15).

A second theme in this passage is the theme of doing ministry, specifically prophetic preaching and praxis, in one's own hometown. Frankly, this is the place where ministry is needed the most. In Luke 4:16, the gospel writer describes Jesus coming back to his hometown for synagogue worship. The narrative describes the setting noting that the geographical locale was Nazareth, the place where Jesus had been reared. This is significant because the emotional impact regarding Jesus' prophetic words and subsequent rejection made it weightier. In fact, Jesus – probably anticipating his hometown rejection – states that prophets are not accepted in their own hometown (v. 24). The Greek word for accepted in v. 24 is the adjective δεκτός (*dektos*) meaning acceptable, favorable or pleasing. This Greek adjective shares the same root with the verb δέχομαι (*dechomai*) which means to take or receive. However, in the context of Luke 4:24, the nuance suggests that while prophets have a hometown, they do not receive a welcome or hospitality practices. Their association with YHWH as a prophet carrying messages of liberation for the socially and economically deprived as well as judgment against the powerholders and their abuse,

---

[45] Stephen Westerholm and Craig A. Evans, "Sabbath" in *The Dictionary of New Testament Background*, eds., Craig A. Evans and Stanley E. Porter (Downers Grove, IL: InterVarsity Press, 2000), 1032.

makes them unwelcomed. The use of the root δέχομαι, however, is used in other places in this text. For instance, in v. 19 as Jesus interprets Isaiah 61 claiming it to be the year of favor, or the acceptable year, he uses the same Greek adjective δέκτος. Here the term is used in a positive sense emphasizing YHWH's redemption of the oppressed as favorable or pleasing through the ministry of Jesus.[46]

This theme can also be expanded to discuss prophets in other parts of Scripture who are rejected and face difficulty while doing prophetic ministry. The prophet Jeremiah is listed among these. Jeremiah, a late 7th century prophet, preached and prophesied to people who rejected his message and put him in physical danger. In Jeremiah 20:1-2, Pashhur who was a priest and high ruling official in the temple, beat Jeremiah because of the content of his prophesies. Then he put him in a holding place until the next day. Jeremiah was also thrown in a cistern because of his prophesies (38:1-6). King Zedekiah gave him over to other civic officials who were offended by his words. This action was to stop Jeremiah's prophetic ministry. However, Ebed-melech an Ethiopian eunuch serving in the king's palace recused him (38:7-12). Amos, the 8th century Judean prophet also faced rejection and difficulty. As a Judean prophet he prophesied in the northern kingdom. However, his prophetic ministry offended the establishment which resulted in a harsh rebuke. In Amos 7:10-17, Amaziah the priest confronted Amos because of his words and accused him of insurrection. Lastly, Elijah the ninth century prophet, prophesied during the time of the Omride dynasty. After defeating the priests of Baal on Mount Carmel, Jezebel issued a death threat against him (1 Kings 18:1-4). This sent Elijah into hiding with depression and suicidal thought until an angel of YHWH comforted him (vv. 5-8).

---

[46] Moisés Silva, "δέχομαι δέκτος," in *The New International Dictionary of New Testament Theology & Exegesis,* vol. 1 (Grand Rapids: Zondervan, 2014), 673.

A third theme in Luke 4:14-30 is the theme of preaching good news to the poor (v. 18). Jesus who functions in the role of prophet and messiah exhibits audacity and courage to preach a message that liberates the oppressed and by implication calls out societal systems of oppression. It also provides healing for the outcasts. The verb for "preaching good news" or "to proclaim" in v. 18 is εὐαγγελίζω (*euangelizo*). It is related to the noun εὐαγγέλιον which means "gospel." The verb occurs 54 times in the New Testament. In Luke-Acts it occurs 25 times, 7 times in the general epistles, 21 times in the Pauline epistles and 1 time in Matthew's gospel. This statistical data shows that the writer of Luke-Acts and Paul used this verb the most. Here the verb occurs in the aorist middle infinite form. Since it is a deponent verb, it always carries an active voice meaning. In Luke's gospel, for instance, the verb is used in a variety of senses. The angel Gabriel brings a message of good news to Zechariah concerning the birth of John the Baptist (1:18-19). After Mary gave birth to Jesus, an angel appeared to Mary and Joseph encouraging them not to fear his presence because he was bringing good news to them (2:10). John the Baptist prepares the way for Jesus by preaching goods news to the people (3:18). Jesus said to various people that his purpose and mission was to preach the good news (4:43).

An important observation regarding the preaching of the good news are the recipients. When Jesus preaches good news, the recipients are those are not part of the establishment. They are people who are not part of the elite in society nor do they have any power to abuse within societal structures—essentially the outcasts.[47] For example, when John the Baptist's disciples went to Jesus asking him about whether he was the messiah, Jesus pointed to the connection between him preaching good news and the evidence of it (7:22; 8:1; 9:6). Preaching the good news

---

[47] Daniel L. Bock, "Luke, Gospel of" in *The Dictionary of Jesus and the Gospels*, ed., Scott McKnight and Joel B. Green (Downers Grove, IL: InterVarsity Press, 1992), 506.

for Jesus is not a message of liberation, but it includes works that change the people's living conditions and socio-economic stigma. In 7:22, the blind receive sight, the lame walk, lepers are cleansed, deaf people here, dead people are raised. However, the verse ends and climaxes with Jesus claiming the poor have the good news.

In the canonical context, this theme can also be expanded to address how the marginalized groups in Scripture are to be dealt with. These groups consistent of the poor, the orphans and widows. They can also be expanded to include women, children, eunuchs (especially since they are treated as outsiders), and the stranger. Space will not allow all these categories to be discussed here. However, it is worth addressing a few. In the Hebrew Bible, people who consist of the poor are described as economically destitute or near financial ruin. They do not have wealth and economic resources in general like the elite and ruling class. The covenant code includes societal responsibility and provisions which acknowledges poor people's existence as well as a means to provide assistance. Exodus 23:11, the law about the seventh year sabbath, instructs the community to leave food in the fields and the vineyards so that the poor and beasts of the fields can eat. Also, there are instructions concerning how a loan to a poor person is to be given. According to Exodus 22:25, a person is not allowed to charge interest on a loan given to a person who is poor. In legal situations, a person is not to twist justice concerning a lawsuit that a poor person brings against them (Exodus 23:6). Similarly, becomes the personal defender of not only the poor, but specifically the widow, the orphan and the stranger within the community (Exodus 22:21-24). If these persons are mistreated, God has promised to hear their cry, cause his anger to burn and kill the person and his family for mistreating them (Exodus 22:23-24).

A fourth theme in this text is doing ministry through the power of the Spirit. As scholars have noted, this is a common theme throughout both Luke and Acts.[48] Mark Strauss rightly observes that the ministry of Jesus in Luke and the ministry of his disciples begins the age in which the Spirit has come.[49] In Luke 4:14-30, Jesus' ministry in Galilee is described with the power of the Spirit (v. 14). His spirit-empowered teaching in the synagogue causes people to praise him and his words (v. 15). This same power of the spirit equipped Jesus to preach the controversial message of liberation in vv. 18-19. It also helped him to escape the attempted assault causing him to leave town (v. 29-30). Prior to our focus text, the Holy Spirit descended upon Jesus at his baptism (3:21-22). The spirit was present with Jesus as he returned from the Jordan (4:1). Also, the Spirit led him to fast in the wilderness for forty days (4:2).

Conclusion

This essay has provided a close reading and exegesis of Isaiah 58:1-14 and Luke 4:16-30, as a foundation for constructing a Black Lives Matter hermeneutic in reading and preaching prophetically. Isaiah 58 becomes fundamentally important because the prophet attacks Judah's liturgical practices in light of its socioeconomic realities. Simply stated, Judah cannot worship YHWH responsibly, if its liturgical practices are rooted in a flawed hermeneutic resulting in theological malfeasance. Judah's flawed hermeneutic consisted of a theological perspective that capitalized off the oppression of the already marginalized within the community. It interpreted its Scripture in ways which neglected its ethnic heritage, its religious tradition grounded in YHWH's character and covenantal values, and the welfare of disadvantaged persons members within the

---

[48] Mark Strauss, "Luke" in *The Zondervan Illustrated Biblical Background Commentary*, vol.1, ed., Clinton Arnold (Grand Rapids: Zondervan, 2002), 329.

[49] Strauss, "Luke," 329.

community. The upper echelon, which remains the dominant voice of the community, prioritized practicing rituals and so-called personal piety while neglecting issues of poverty, homelessness, physical violence—possibly gang violence—unfair wage and labor practices, and unethical business transactions. The persons responsible for this behavior and those who were able to change it were the priests and the upper-class. The theological presuppositions of the upper-class suggested that seeking YHWH's ways alone was enough to fulfill their covenant obligation. It suggested that YHWH was concerned only with the dominant culture to the exclusion of the disadvantaged.

YHWH spoke through the prophet to address Judah's theological malfeasance and their hegemonic and religious practices. This is important because Isaiah 58 addresses the issue of justice and righteousness throughout the entire book. Since this paper presupposes three Isaiahs in three different time periods for three different communities, it posits that even in the eight, sixth and possibly fifth centuries, Isaiah and the Isaianic disciples or Isaianic school of prophets struggled to understand and practice justice as a fundamental expression of its worship and interpersonal relationships.

Since preaching is part of worship within the Christian tradition, Isaiah 58 serves as a warning and a corrective. Like Judah's worship practice, much contemporary Black preaching, and liturgical practices are rife with hermeneutical hegemony and theological malfeasance. The focus on one's own interest, brazen exclusivity within the community and the neglect of the black church's reason for existence comes out in much black preaching. This passage serves as a model for this project in creating a curriculum to address contextual issues of injustice, hegemonic structures within and outside of the Black church community and a sustained focus on integrating social justice and preaching as an important part of the Black church's liturgical practice.

Luke 4:16-30 echoes some themes within Isaiah 58, which makes it equally foundational for this project. For instance, Jesus' choice of text and reading from the Isaiah scroll highlights themes of justice, the concept of the year of jubilee and the concern for the disadvantage is consistent with Isaiah 58. Here Jesus shows compassion on and gives priority and voice to persons who are blind (physically), economically destitute, victims of the inequities of the criminal justice system, and others who are taken advantage of by the dominant culture's self-interest and quest for socioeconomic gain at the expense of others. He announces his mission and purpose as combining issues of justice and liturgical practice in a new context, which in Luke's gospel highlights Jesus' favor on those who are outcasts in society.

Jesus uses the liturgical practice of Scripture reading and proclamation combined with a radical theopraxis to challenge religious leaders to renounce civil religion in order to see, hear and perform justice. Also, he challenges the common person, the listeners, through his model to go and do likewise. The ability to accomplish this comes through the Spirit of the Lord, which focuses on addressing social injustices. As a result, this passage helps to establish the purpose and agenda of biblical interpretation and preaching as that which addresses social injustice which is consistent with the gospel Jesus preached.

BIBLIOGRAPHY

Achtemeier, Elizabeth. *The Community and Message of Isaiah 56-66: A Theological Commentary*. Minneapolis: Augsburg Publishing, 1982.

Bennett, Harold V. "Justice, OT." In *The New Interpreter's Dictionary of the Bible*. Vol. 3, edited by Katherine Doob Sakenfeld, 476-477. Nashville: Abingdon Press, 2009.

Blenkinsopp, Joseph. *Isaiah 40-55*. The Anchor Bible. New York: Doubleday, 2002.

_____. *Isaiah 56-66: A New Translation with Introduction and Commentary*. Anchor Bible, Vol. 19b. New York: Doubleday, 2003.

Bock, Darrell L. "Luke, Gospel of." In *The Dictionary of Jesus and the Gospels,* edited by Joel B. Green and Scot McKnight, 495-510. Downers Grove: InterVarsity Press, 1992.

_____. Luke Volume 1: 1:1-9:50. Baker Exegetical Commentary on the New Testament. Grand Rapids: Baker Books, 2002.

Childs, Brevard. *Isaiah*. The Old Testament Library. Louisville: Westminster John Knox Press, 2001.

Clifford, Richard. "Isaiah Book of." In *The New Interpreter's Dictionary of the Bible*. Vol. 3, edited by Katherine Doob Sakenfeld, 75-91. Nashville: Abingdon Press, 2009.

Coogan, Michael D. *The Old Testament: A Historical and Literary Introduction to the Hebrew Bible*. Oxford: Oxford University Press, 2011.

Croatto, J. Severino. "Isaiah 56-66." In *Global Bible Commentary,* edited by Daniel Patte, 201-206. Nashville: Abingdon Press, 2004.

deSilva, David. *An Introduction to the New Testament: Contexts, Methods & Ministry Formation*. Downers Grove: InterVarsity Press, 2004.

Emerson, Grace I. *Isaiah 56-66*. Old Testament Guides. Sheffield: Sheffield Academic Press, 1992.

Goldingay, John. *The Theology of the Book of Isaiah*. Downers Grove, IL: IVP Academic, 2014.

Gorman, Michael J. *Elements of Biblical Exegesis: A Basic Guide for Students and Ministers*. Revised edition. GrandRapids: Baker Academic, 2009.

Green, Joel B. *The Gospel of Luke*. The New International Commentary on the New Testament. Grand Rapids: William B. Eerdmans, 1997.

Hayes, Elizabeth R. "Justice, Righteousness." In *The Dictionary of the Old Testament Prophets*, edited by Mark J. Boda and J. Gordon McConville, 466-472. Downers Grove: InterVarsity Press, 2012.

Irwin, Brian P. "Social Justice." In *The Dictionary of the Old Testament Prophets,* edited by Mark J. Boda and J. Gordon McConville, 719-734. Downers Grove: InterVarsity Press, 2012.

Klein, William W., Craig L. Blomberg, and Robert L. Hubbard. *Introduction to Biblical Interpretation.* Revised edition. Nashville: Thomas Nelson Publishers, 1993.

Lambert, David A. "Fast, Fasting." In *The New Interpreter's Dictionary of the Bible.* Vol. 2, edited by Katherine Doob Sakenfeld, 431-434. Nashville: Abingdon Press, 2009.

LaSor, William Sanford, David Allen Hubbard and Frederic William Bush. *Old Testament Survey: The Message, Form and Background of the Old Testament.* 2nd edition. Grand Rapids: Eerdmans, 1996.

Jenson, Philip P. "Temple." In *The Dictionary of the Old Testament Prophets,* edited by Mark J. Boda and J. Gordon McConville, 767-775. Downers Grove: InterVarsity Press, 2012.

Johnson, Luke Timothy. *The Gospel of Luke.* Sacra Pagina Series, Vol. 3. Collegeville, MN: The Liturgical Press, 1991.

Niskanen, Paul V. *Isaiah 56-66.* Berit Olam Studies in Hebrew & Narrative Poetry. Collegeville, Minnesota: The Liturgical Press, 2014.

Oswalt, John. *Isaiah.* The NIV Application Commentary. Grand Rapids: Zondervan, 2003.

Paul, Shalom. *Isaiah 40-66: Translation and Commentary.* Eerdmans Critical Commentary. Louisville: Westminster John Knox Press, 2012.

Ringe, Sharon H. "Jubilee, Year of." In *The New Interpreter's Dictionary of the Bible.* Vol. 3, edited by Katherine Doob Sakenfeld, 418-419. Nashville: Abingdon Press, 2009.

Schiffman, Lawrence H. "Torah." In *The New Interpreter's Dictionary of the Bible.* Vol. 5, edited by Katherine Doob Sakenfeld, 629-630. Nashville: Abingdon Press, 2009.

Silva, Moisés. "δέχομαι δέκτος," in *The New International Dictionary of New Testament Theology & Exegesis.* Vol. 1. Grand Rapids: Zondervan, 2014.

Sloan, Robert B. "Jubilee." In *The Dictionary of Jesus and the Gospels,* edited by Joel B. Green and Scot McKnight, 396-397. Downers Grove: InterVarsity Press, 1992.

Strauss, Mark. "Luke." In *The Zondervan Illustrated Biblical Background Commentary.* Vol. 1, edited by Clinton Arnold, 318-502. Grand Rapids: Zondervan, 2002.

Sweeney, Marvin A. "Form Criticism." In *To Each its Own Meaning: An Introduction to Biblical Criticisms and their Application.* Revised and Expanded, edited by Steven McKenzie and Stephen Hayes, 58-89. Louisville: Westminster John Knox Press, 1999.

_____. *Isaiah 1-39 with an Introduction to Prophetic Literature.* The Forms of The Old Testament Literature, Vol. 16. Grand Rapids: Eerdmans, 1996.

Watson, Wilfred G.E. *Classical Hebrew Poetry: A Guide to its Techniques.* New York: T&T Clark International, 2005.

Westerholm, Stephen and Craig A. Evans. "Sabbath." In *The Dictionary of New Testament Background,* edited by Craig A. Evans and Stanley E. Porter, 1031-1035. Downers Grove: InterVarsity Press, 2000.

Vorster, Willem S. "Gospel Genre." In *Anchor Yale Bible Dictionary.* Vol. 2, edited by David Noel Freeman, 1077-1079. Nashville: Abingdon Press, 2009.

Whybray, R. N. *The Second Isaiah.* Old Testament Guides. Sheffield: Sheffield Academic Press, 1997.

Yamauchi, Edwin. "Synagogue." In *The Dictionary of Jesus and the Gospels,* edited by Joel B. Green and Scot McKnight, 781-784. Downers Grove: InterVarsity Press, 1992.

THE AFRICAN AMERICAN CHURCH: A WORKING DEFINITION

Rev. Kurt S. Clark, D.Min.

The African American church[1] has always been the locus, or epicenter, for redemptive preaching and the reclamation and liberation of the true concept of *imago Dei* (that all men are made in the image of God). It has been the primordial context for alternative existence and free-standing prophecy against the oppressive structures of a dominant community, vis-à-vis America as empire.[2] As such the African American church has always been a model *subcommunity*.[3] It has been the operatic voice in opposing the hegemony of American imperialism, not ceasing its assertions of the longstanding injustices of white America against the black community. In poem and peroration it has been ever so diligent in reminding the dominant community of its unconscionable deeds. Walter Brueggemann observed in his text *The Word Militant*,

> "I/*we, the black church*, [emphasis mine] say things long known. We keep saying them to each other, because if they are left unsaid, the old powers of death creep back in and take over. We say them to each other, because we depend on the fresh

---

[1] When I speak of the African American church I mean an institution whose origin was the locus for an alternative existence. To this end I make reference to the era of the "invisible institution" (the hush harbor) when both free and enslaved Negro believers would steal away into the thickets to worship authentically and to hear in black voice the gospel narrative interpreted in light of their struggle, therefore fostering an alternative reality. It was in the hush harbor that they also planned for revolt upon hearing the gospel proclaimed in a way that they envisioned themselves as the new Israel and the slave masters as the Philistines. Thusly, the hush harbor became the incubator for an alternative existence that is apart from the empire. Its primal practices have been those of preaching, re-imaging, and other forms of prophetic activity by which it challenges, juxtaposes, and confronts the oppressive practices of the more dominant community. The African American church and its praxes offer unto the ear, eye, and imagination an alternative reality, one of justice-oriented ethos and equality of kinship apart from race, ethnicity, religiosity, economic status, or gender.

[2] For the purpose of this paper, when I speak of empire I mean the American hegemonic (culturally dominating) system that practices the oppressive and invasive traditions of empire.

[3] When I speak about the African American church as subcommunity I mean a community that stands in opposition to its dominating community and its cultural practices of empire.

utterance to give fresh edge of possibility to our lives. We say these things to each other, because the utterances mediate the Easter option . . . without utterance, no such option.

The sense of this utterance, in which we/*the black church* [emphasis mine] are participants, is that an alternative world is possible. The old world is not a given; it is a fraud. Another world is possible—in our imagination: We listen and imagine differently. In our liberation, we entertain different realities not yet given in hardware, so far only in very-soft-ware, carried only by narrative and song and poem and oracle, said before being embodied, but said and we listen. As we listen, we push out to the possibility and are held by it like a visioning child with a dream.[4]

As a people who were only propelled by the mere software of new possibilities and unbound dreams, the African American church as subcommunity knew of other possibilities beyond the hardware of their present reality. As avant-garde, the African American church as sect and subcommunity would push out to the utter edge of new possibilities. Fighting for freedoms and desiring equality, the African American church has since its unusual origin championed causes of liberation, justice, and freedom, thus presenting itself as a kind of surrogate presence, an alternative existence, effecting transformative leadership within the African American community.

In Brueggemann's text, *The Prophetic Imagination*, Brueggemann expounds on the inherent power of the imagination as a precursor to alternative existence and radical prophetic activity. The African American church has championed the cause in preaching prophetically, often with very few resources to its credit. However, in the words of Brueggemann when commenting on Phyllis Trible's *God and the Rhetoric of Sexuality*, the African American church has understood the value of imagination as "a legitimate *and indispensable* [emphasis mine] way of knowing."[5] In William R. Herzog's *Prophet*

---

[4] Walter Brueggemann, *The Word Militant: Preaching a Decentering Word* (Minneapolis: Fortress Press, 2007), 165.

[5] Walter Brueggemann, *The Prophetic Imagination* (Minneapolis: Fortress Press, 2001), x.

and Teacher, Herzog noted a revelatory moment of Paulo Freire when studying and working with the village peasants in Brazil. Herzog states,

> When Freire began his work with the peasant villagers, he discovered that they were under the spell of an ideology that had been impressed upon them and implanted in them by the ruling class of Brazil. In this "social construction of reality," peasants were little more than objects in their oppressors' reality with no history to call their own past), no way make sense of their own experience (present), and no vocation to remake their world (future). Rather they were locked in an eternally unchanging and hopeless present. Freire discovered that the peasants with whom he was working had internalized the world of their oppressors and, as they did, they were submerging themselves into a self-imposed culture of silence in which they had neither voice nor vision ....Freire decided that, in order to teach these peasants to read, he first had to teach them how to read their world and diagnose their condition.[6]

While African Americans were initially without the benefit of being taught how to read, they were skilled in the art of cultural hermeneutics of interpreting their own socio- economic, political, and cultural realities—their new world. They were able to read the disparities that existed between them and their enslaver—between what they said and what they did in light of their socio-religious doctrines. In his text *Jesus and Empire*, Richard Horsley commented on the slaves' inability to read texts: "Although not permitted to learn to read, African American slaves, when they heard the biblical stories of the Israelites' exodus from bondage and the promised land to which God guided them, fantasized/*imagined* escaping from slavery and "goin' over Jordan" to the promised land of freedom."[7] The African American church/community[8] made sense of its new world

---

[6] William R. Herzog II, *Prophet and Teacher* (Louisville, Kentucky: Westminster John Knox Press, 2005), 17.

[7] Richard A. Horsley, ed., *Jesus and Empire: The Kingdom of God and the New World Order* (Minneapolis: Fortress Press, 2003), 1.

[8] E. Franklin Frazier and C. Eric Lincoln, *The Negro Church in America* and *The Black Church Since Frazier* (New York: Schocken Books, 1974), 115. I speak of the African American church with great deference to C. Eric Lincoln's distinction of it as being indistinguishable from the black community. He

disorder[9] in light of its ontology, its blackness, and prophetically imagined a better day—an alternative. Brueggemann envisioned a better day as being energizing and forceful because the alternative, or subcommunity, dares to affirm—prophetically—how the future will turn out.[10] When African American church historian Henry Mitchell reflected on the slaves' account of gross injustices and disparities within the African American disfavored world of "slavocracy," he shared of the Word's effect on the enslaved to anticipate an alternative and to bring about a change.

> Meanwhile, a few slaves illegally learned to read the whole Bible, and others just heard the Word and retained it. They then selected the parts that strengthened them and gave them *hope*. Thus, when they read what Paul said in Galatians 6:7 about people reaping what they sow, this law of identical harvest was easily accepted because it had been previously taught in African traditional religion. In addition, they were especially fond of the part about people who do good reaping in "due season" (6:9). In fact, that theme of due season is still greatly cherished in the African American pulpit, because of the help and *hope* it still gives oppressed people.[11]

The correlating thoughts and images of freedom, parity, and retribution were natural conjurings of the Word's ability to effect change and to bring about an alternative reality that was radically different from the one inhabited. As the Bible conjured up feelings and images of reversal and alternative, the African American church waited and worked for an alternative reality, one of justice and equality, apart from race, ethnicity, gender, and socioeconomic status.

---

saw no disjunction between the black church and the black community. For Lincoln the black church was the spiritual face of the black community, thus there is no disunity suggested by the use of the two.

[9] Horsley, *Jesus and Empire: The Kingdom of God and the New World Disorder*, 4.

[10] Walter Brueggemann, *The Prophetic Imagination* (Minneapolis: Fortress Press, 2001), 15.

[11] Henry H. Mitchell, *Black Church Beginnings: The Long-Hidden Realities of the First Years* (Grand Rapids: Eerdmans Publishing Company, 2004), 16.

David Hogue believe that "Imagination is the stage on which we play out what could be the field of spontaneous play where the limitations of the real world are suspended for a time."[12] In it, Hogue says, "We make our way to relief and escape—or sometimes to scenes of anxiety or terror,"[13] all of which are contrivances of the imagination.

In Brian Blount's text *Then the Whisper Put on Flesh*, Blount remarks on the slaves' creative and uncanny ability *as a subcommunity* [emphasis mine] to use tasks such as shucking corn as a time of controlled escapism and countercultural resistance.[14] Blount says, "In those controlled 'fun times' slaves dreamed the counter dreams of resistance and liberty."[15] He also declares that "The slaves stole pleasure, co-opted power, and appropriated resources in an effort to foster self-respect and engineer a sense of their access to such fundamental human rights; they were trafficking in the black market of resistance. Even activities that on the surface appeared to be innocuous, 'fun' events of escapist pleasure had their way of seeding spiritual and, quite often, physical dissent."[16] As a community which traffics in the black market of resistance and stands in tension with the larger and dominant community, the African American church clearly establishes itself as veritable subcommunity.

---

[12] David A. Hogue, *Remembering the Future Imagining The Past: Story, Ritual, and the Human Brain* (Eugene, Oregon: Wipf & Stock, 2003), 14.

[13] Ibid.

[14] Brian K. Blount, *Then the Whisper Put on Flesh: New Testament Ethics in an African American Context* (Nashville: Abingdon Press, 2001), 95.

[15] Ibid.

[16] Ibid.

Unequivocally, and perhaps even before social scientists and psychologists fully understood its effect, the black church realized the value and promise of imagination[17] as a temporary suspension of reality with attendant hopes of a reversal and alternative. Although Brueggemann has been instrumental in naming the intricacies of prophetic ministry, the African American church since its inception in America has positioned itself and carried out practices consistent with that of an authentic prophetic guild, or subcommunity. Brueggemann's view of a subcommunity out of which prophetic activity hails unequivocally bespeaks the history and activity of the African American church.

The very essence of Brueggemann's description of a subcommunity reflects the history of the African American church—its ecclesiology and sociology—within the throes of a dominant America as empire. Brueggemann describes the existence of a subcommunity as one in which . . .

- there is a *long and available memory* that sinks the present generation deep into an identifiable past that is available in song and story;

- there is an available, expressed *sense of pain* that is owned and recited as a real social fact, that is visibly acknowledged in a public way, and that is understood as unbearable for the long term;

- there is an *active practice of hope*, a community that knows about promises yet to be kept, promises that stand in judgment on the present;

- there is an *effective mode of discourse* that is cherished across the generations, that is taken as distinctive, and that is richly coded in ways that only insiders can know.[18]

The characteristics and traits that are indigenous to subcommunity are clearly present and embodied within African American church and community—its ecclesiology

---

[17] For the purpose of this paper, terms such as "imagined," "re-creation," and "co-constitution"—terms of cognition—are often used interchangeably as a part of the *re-imaging* praxis of the African American church.

[18] Brueggeman, *The Prophetic Imagination*, xvi.

and sociology. With these realities I unreservedly offer the African American church as subcommunity—a thinkable mode of ministry.[19]

Its Origins and Mission

In sync with Brueggemann's characterization of a prophetic subcommunity—a community that stands in tension with the dominant community in any political economy—are specific moments, watershed events, that gave rise to the African American church as veritable subcommunity. Examples are the long night of slavery, the height of the civil rights movement, and the continued neglect of systems that are disadvantageous toward the life of the African American community. Dwight N. Hopkins commented on the origin of that which gave rise to the subcommunity and its theology.

> Poor black folk created their own faith in the hell of over two hundred years of slavery. Despite being the private property of slave masters, despite being torn from their African homeland and ripped away from parents and other family members, African Americans enjoyed the beauty of a faith which maintained their humanity and their hope in a new *alternative* [emphasis mine] heaven and a new earth for their children.
>
> From the seventh to nineteenth century, African and African American enslaved workers constructed a new religion *a new community* [emphasis mine] drawing on three sources—memories of African religious beliefs, commonsense wisdom from everyday life, and a reinterpretation of the white-supremacy Christianity introduced to them by their Christian slave masters. The cornerstone of a black theology of liberation was thus a slave religion of freedom.[20]

It was in the midst of such mammoth despair and dehumanization that Africans as a disenfranchised community formed themselves into a subcommunity, i.e., a thinkable mode of ministry. They remembered their African religious beliefs, and they re-interpreted their enslavers' supremacist Christianity while simultaneously trying to make

---

[19] Ibid, xvii.

[20] Dwight N. Hopkins, *Introducing Black Theology of Liberation* (Maryknoll, New York: Orbis Books, 1999), 16.

sense of an undesirable and disfavored reality. Hopkins believes that it was during the times in underground worship—the invisible institution, the hush harbor—that "Blacks recreated themselves with God."[21] Such recreation, *re-imaging* and co-constitution of itself empowered the community to believe in an alternative that was unlike their present reality.

Despite the recreation of the self as subcommunity, the African American church could not afford to go to sleep at the helm or diminish its vigilance. Issues of civil injustices were yet unresolved, and the African American church as subcommunity would have to become the watchtower for justice and the hub (primordial context) for liberation and reclamation—the alternative.

Brueggemann observes that a prophet, as a constituent of the subcommunity, is free to focus on his role and mission within the subcommunity. As Brueggemann explains, God is at liberty to make of whom He wants as prophet when and wherever He wishes, but certain environs are less hospitable to prophets than others.[22] In such case, Brueggemann joins with Robert Wilson in describing the prophet as "peripheral" when he stands in opposition to authorities and establishments of the dominant culture. This view of the prophet as peripheral has been the very context and the psychogenesis, the beginning, out of which the African American preacher has emerged. The involuntary presence of a people in America naturally created for itself a kind of mutual resentment and resistance. Out of that grew a sustained resistance as the subcommunity began to develop its voice within the sociopolitical realities of which they were undeniably a part.

---

[21] Ibid.

[22] Brueggemann, *The Prophetic Imagination*, xvi.

The black preacher began to preach justice and freedom and parity as persons whose presence was involuntary and whose personhood was denied. This created for itself a culture of resistance and rebellion that was often misunderstood as savagery and barbarity—although this barbarity was more like the gross theft of a people from their native land. Despite the misnomer of such activity that was undeniably spurred on and perpetuated by black "peripheral" prophets, their interest was that of the complete human, bodily, and historical existence of their people.[23] Prophets such as Nat Turner, Denmark Vesey, Gabriel Prosser, Henry McNeal Turner, Harriet Tubman, Sojourner Truth, and David Walker were just a few who rose as phoenix from the ash heaps of dehumanization and injustice.

The African American church has been the seedbed for such blossoming figures who have not sought prominence, prestige, or celebrity status. Theirs was the universal justice of God within His created order. Despite the recent celebrated status of such historical figures within the black community, prophets were persons through whom the community developed a certain consciousness and an ability to suffer and endure pain.[24] In Martin King's embrace of Gandhi's nonviolence philosophy, many in the South and in other places literally developed a capacity and a prophetic consciousness to suffer.

Interesting too is one's ability to suffer even liturgically by way of the Eucharist. In Brueggemann's account of Cavanaugh's *Torture and Eucharist: Theology, Politics and the Body of Christ*, Brueggemann believes the Eucharist to be a community-forming miracle and vehicle for the rule and subsequent kingdom of God as well as a practical instrument for generating communities of resistance against the state.[25] One such characteristic of a *peripheral prophet* (as one who creates a consciousness of pain within subcommunity) is no novelty in the life of the African American church, but normal instead. In fact, its very birth was one of pain—a natural process. In his chapter of *The Courage To Hope*, Albert J. Raboteau comments on the mystery of the slaves' ability to endure suffering as it took on new meaning in light of Jesus' suffering:

> I could no hab libbed had not been for de Lord…neber! Work so late, and so early; work so hard, when side ache so. Chil'en sold; old man gone. All visitors, and company in big house; all cooking and washing all on me, neber done enough. Missus neber satisfied—no hope. Nothing, nothing but Jesus, I look up. O Lord! how long? Give me patience! Patience! O Lord! only Jesus know how bad I feel; darsn't tell any body, else get flogged. Darsn't call upon de Lord; darsn't tell when sick. But…I said Jesus, if it your will, I will bear it.[26]

The African American church as subcommunity has not only made its entrée into the grander scheme of the dominant community by creating a consciousness of suffering and pain but also by availing itself of its "thinkable" ministry and its powerful imagination. The African American church in its beginning saw itself as something other than what it was said to be and *imagined* a reality that was different from its present. The envisioning and imaginative process was without exception manufactured by the creative preaching of the black preacher. Such sermons as that of the late Rev. John Jasper "De Sun Do Move" without the benefit of science moved the black church into understanding something of the nature of God through imaginative preaching. Preaching of this sort was

---

[25] Ibid, xix.

[26] Dixie, Quinton Hosford and Cornel West, eds. *The Courage To Hope: From Black Suffering to*

prophetic in that it energized the community, and it permitted a people to live inside of God's imagination and not that of the oppressor, the dominant community.[27]

African American preaching has always offered itself as a medium for achieving reclamation and liberation of the true concept of *imago Dei* and *God's*. It has presented this reality within a culture of highly imaginative preaching—preaching which awakens in the hearer the awareness of an alternative reality than that of the dominant culture.[28] Preaching of this sort sprang forth from the imagination of prophetic preachers who were part of the imaginative community which viewed/imagined itself as a people of God amid systems that were unrelenting in declaring otherwise. As an oppressed community whose presence was involuntary and unwelcome, the black church used as fodder for its faith imaginative stories as that of "High John de Conquer," who according to Brian K. Blount was "a black-messiah man, a deliverer, who despite the horrors of present reality, conjured up trust for a better tomorrow."[29] Such folkloric myths were essential and indispensible for sustained faith and ultimate triumph. It was against such dismal backdrop of oppression, slavery and discrimination that the black preacher painted Rembrandt- and Picasso-like images of an imagined future. According to Blount, High John de Conquer was a pocket of faith who helped those enslaved peoples *the imagined community* [emphasis mine] survive.

> High John de Conquer came to be a man, and a mighty man at that. But he was not a natural man in the beginning. First off, he was a whisper, a will to hope, a wish to find something worthy of laughter and song. Then the whisper put on flesh. His footsteps sounded across the world in a low but musical rhythm as if the world he walked on was a singing drum. The black folks had an irresistible

---

[27] Brueggemann, xx.

[28] Ibid, 3.

[29] Brian K. Blount, *Go Preach! Mark's Kingdom Message and the Black Church Today* (Maryknoll, New York: Orbis Books, 1998), 3.

> impulse to laugh. High John de Conquer was a man in full, and had come to live and work on the plantations, and all the slave folks knew him in the flesh.
>
> The sign of this man was a laugh, and his singing symbol was a drum beat. No parading drum shout like soldiers out for show. It did not call to the feet of those who were fixed to hear it. It was an inside thing to live by. It was sure to be heard when and where the work was the hardest, and the lot most cruel. It helped the slaves endure. They knew that something better was coming. So they laughed in the face of things and sang, "I'm so glad! Trouble don't last always."[30]

Such stories energized the hearers who were inclined to understand the Morse code of folkloric language and who understood the necessity and promise of prophetic imagination. People who were oppressed by the disadvantages of the dominant system would come to know the advantages and power of imaginative reality. As clarified by Brian K. Blount, "High John de Conquer is a projection of power, an objective 'story' manifestation of a subjective belief, a force of thought that intervened in the spiritual reality of human life and represented a future possibility of freedom and respect that did not exist in the present."[31] The black church as imaginative subcommunity proffered itself as an anti-imperial movement in countering uncritical claims of the dominant community. It gave rise prophetically to a hope and reason to press beyond the present fraudulent realities in an anticipation of one which was to come. As imaginative voice in countering critical claims of the greater dominant community, the black church could not allow for apathy. Numbness does not hurt like torture, but in a quite parallel way it robs of capability.[32] Prophetically, black imaginative preaching always insisted on the right to be full spiritual and material human beings.[33] Imagination is that upon which the African

---

[30] Ibid.

[31] Ibid, 4.

[32] Brueggeman, *The Prophetic Imagination*, xx.

[33] Dwight N. Hopkins, *Down, Up and Over: Slave Religion and Black Theology* (Minneapolis: Fortress Press, 2000), 6.

American church as subcommunity has constantly seized in order to live within the reality of God's imagination. Therefore, African American preaching *is* prophetic and imaginative because it reaches out beyond the ordinary and the reasonable.[34]

Commenting on the power of the imagination, David Hogue said, "Our imaginations are another thing altogether—at least as we normally think of imagination. Imagination is less concerned with what is, or has been, than with what could be. It is less concerned with established facts and more with possibility…imagination calls on the absurd or at least the nonrational. Stories or events or relationships that are impossible in the real world *can work*—and even make sense—in the wonderful world of the imagination."[35]

Although the African American church as subcommunity has benefited from a culture of highly imaginative preaching, there are other aspects of prophetic activity through which the grace of God has been mediated. In Wilda C. Gafney's *Daughters of Miriam,* she asserts that there are many prophetic mediums through which the graces of God can be mediated. Gafney's research on the roles of prophecy in early Israelite history reveals multiple modes of mediation that were prophetic in Israel some of which includes dancing, drumming, praying, singing, and teaching.[36] Gafney's working definition of prophecy is "the proclamation and/or performance of a divine word by a religious

---

[34] Brueggemann, *The Prophetic Imagination*, xv.

[35] Hogue, *Remembering the Future, Imagining the Past*, 13.

[36] Wilda C. Gafney, *Daughters of Miriam: Women Prophets in Ancient Israel* (Minneapolis: Fortress Press, 2008), 24.

intermediary to an individual or community."[37] She also states that such activity occurred at the instigation of either humans or deities.

Within the African American church as subcommunity is the vast medium of prophetic activity which is not conventionally seen as such. Thus, I have assigned it the nomenclature of "subculture." For instance, Gafney describes the activity of Ezekiel lying on his side for more than 390 days as prophetic.[38] Such revelations are key for a holistic approach and view of prophetic ministry in naming their origin and intent within the African American context and subcommunity. As Gafney abstains from ranking prophetic ministry in some kind of hierarchical order, I have done so only to note the prevalence of the more traditional view of prophetic ministry—forth-telling and foretelling.

Consistent with the host of prophetic subculture activity of Ancient Israel are sources of theological significance in the development of a black theology of liberation, which too stands in tension with the dominant community in any political economy.

Dwight Hopkins gives a more concise definition of black theology of liberation: "Black theology of liberation is a systematic and constructive movement arising from the reality of God's liberation power existing in all parts of life."[39] As a result, for the slave and African American community there was not bifurcation of soul and spirit or of sacred and secular. Salvation hinged on full human, spiritual, and material freedom.

Like the subculture of prophetic activity of ancient Israel, the sources of black theology are unique in that there is no shared homogeneity with the larger dominant

---

[37] Ibid, 25.

[38] Ibid, 24.

[39] Hopkins, *Introducing Black Theology of Liberation*, 42.

community. Black theology has sources which have spoken to and share with its community out of their own or similar experience. Hopkins says, "In black theology, sources answer the question about the location of the meeting between divine revelation and black humanity."[40] For instance, the Bible clearly speaks of the enslavement of Israel as something with which the African American church can identify. The creation of such stories and the *Sitz im Leben* (life situation) of African Americans lend themselves as usable resources in the creation and articulation of a black theology. Despite the unpleasantness of such a painful past, the promise of exodus instills the African American church with unflappable hope. Hopkins declares,

> Moreover, the African American poor, reading the Hebrew Scriptures from their position on the bottom of American society, discover a whole new world different from the dominating Christianity and theology of mainstream American believers. The exodus theme does not end with harsh difficulties. On the contrary, the hope of deliverance cancels out the pain and gives today's poor the strength to "keep on keeping on." The certainty of victory, witnessed to in the Hebrew Scriptures, gives the poor strength in the midst of their deepest self-doubt caused by seemingly insurmountable odds.
> Likewise, the black poor bring their own contextual concerns to the Christian Scriptures. And Jesus meets and greets them as their liberator, as the one who can perform miracles—turning "the impossible into the possible."[41]

That others aren't able to identify with the exodus liberation motif is no deterrent to the African American community. It is merely one of the convincing sources of reversal and alternative.

Another source of black liberation theology that is unique and clearly part of a subculture of theological sources within the African American church is culture—art, literature, music, folktales, black English, and rhythm.[42] According to Hopkins,

---
[40] Ibid.
[41] Ibid.
[42] Ibid, 45.

> Liberation motifs in nonexplicit Christian texts have always been with African Americans. For example, the heroic and courageous stories about Anansi the Spider—a small, weak creature able to outsmart those with power—were brought by slaves from the west coast of Africa to America's slave colonies and were passed orally from one generation to another. Jazz served periodically as a creative and unique form of protest, refusing to fit within prescribed styles and themes of European- and Euro-American controlled music. Black peoples' specific approach to sports, which takes place when black athletes celebrate with their in-your-face flair, is a unique way of declaring "I am Somebody" in a world controlled by others of a different class and color.. A liberating culture is vital for a constructive black theology.[43]

As voices within subcommunity, it is imperative for prophetic figures to know something of the extensive, elaborate, and eclectic base from which its community derives its theology. The African American church as subcommunity has long used both conventional and nonconventional ways of expressing itself as a means of liberation, reclamation, and protest. The African American church, in giving expression to the breadth and creativity of its thoughts and beliefs, is believable and has developed a body of extracanonical idioms and expressions. In the words of Gregory M. Howard, "Folk theology is theology that a community of people treasures and lives by that is expressed in folklore. Black Christian folklore is expressive culture that includes tales, music, dance, popular beliefs, proverbs, and oral traditions as transmitters of Black folk theology. Black preaching is constituent of Black folklore."[44] The sources of a black theology of liberation are as many and varied as that of the prophetic activity of ancient Israel. There is no single source from which the African American community derives its theology of black liberation, since liberation is a matter of interest in every aspect of life.

---

[43] Ibid.

[44] Gregory M. Howard, *Black Sacred Rhetoric: A Commentary for African American Preaching* (South Carolina: Booksurge Publishing, 2008), 6.

For instance, the African American church has spoken not only in defense of itself regarding apparent injustices, but also for those who were at times not able or accustomed to speaking for themselves against the more dominant culture. In Christine Marie Smith's *Preaching Justice*,[45] she covers an array of justice-oriented issues that are often complex and complicated and even neglected within and without the church.

Included in Smith's book Teresa Fry Brown's article "An African American Woman's Perspective." Brown (with the benefit of Zora Neale Hurston's imagery) rightly identifies the harsh realities of being part of a subcommunity and a victim of the dominant community in any political economy. Brown recounts the years of gender discrimination against her as an African American female who was often denied the right of personhood in exercising her God-given right to preach. Such refusal of right and denial of personhood was antithetical to the voice and creation of subcommunity. Brown notes,

> The disheartening reality is that for most African American women preachers, there is a debilitating conflict between being under orders from God to preach from that weary throat and constantly hearing the voices of the brothers and sisters challenging one's authenticity. The hope for most women preachers is that the freedom of which they preach will come afterwhile…Rooted in the cultural imperative that all must be free, the Black church began in woods, swamps, caves, and secret places of institutional slavery in the early centuries of the Americas. The continuing struggle for a space to worship God who affirmed their personhood and the dominion of all creation led to protests, walkouts, and "stealing away to Jesus."…The difficulty arose when those who made up the institution began their own form of oppression of another group within its walls that might not fit the model…The cognitive dissonance of proclaiming freedom for all, yet continuing to enslave some, is curious.[46]

For Brown the African American church is at times both the "peaky mountain" and "sorrow's kitchen," one of which represents the blessedness of equality and the other

---

[45] Christine Marie Smith, ed., *Preaching Justice: Ethnic and Cultural Perspectives* (Eugene, Oregon: Wipf & Stock, 1998), 43.
[46] Ibid, 44.

the bane of inequality. As subcommunity the African American church must at times stand in tension with itself as it is constantly under the threat of being co-opted by the powers and persuasion of the dominant community. The African American church as subcommunity struggles to succeed in "renovating sorrow's kitchen."[47] The work that it calls for is that of both church and academy in addressing the systemic evils against, women, the disabled, gays and lesbians, foreigners, Native Americans, and the like within the marginalized sector of a dominant culture, vis-à-vis empire. In many ways the African American church has led the way in charting a course for addressing ills that disallow the full embrace of humanity and perpetuate dehumanization.

As cultural anthropologists and those who have an inborn sensitivity to injustices of all kinds, the African American church must not jettison or abandon its place of call in exchange for a few of Pharaoh's concessions. The work of the church and its peripheral prophets is to communicate the possibilities that are revealed with the community's text as an alternative reality and achievable possibility. Brueggemann says of his analysis of literary study,

> In this method, one pays attention to the power of language to propose an imaginative world that is an alternative to the one that seems to be at hand—alternative to the one in which the reader or listener thinks herself or himself enmeshed. Literature then is not regarded as descriptive of what is, but as evocative and constructive of another life world. In this method, one takes the "world" offered in the text as a possible alternative world without excessive reference to historical factors and without excessive interest in authorship. This approach permits literature to be enormously daring and bold, and often abrasive and subversive in the face of the presumed world of the listener. It places the listener in crisis, but also presents the listener with a new zone for fresh hope, changed conduct, and fresh historical possibility.[48]

---

[47] Ibid.

[48] Brueggemann, *A Commentary on Jeremiah: Exile and Homecoming* (Grand Rapids, Michigan: Eerdmans Publishing Company, 1998), 15.

The African American church with continued diligence will no doubt continue countering structures and systems of injustices which are both within and without— renovating sorrow's kitchen—as they threaten humanity and perpetuate dehumanization. As J. Deotis Roberts says of Jesus' ministry, "His ministry was a public ministry, in that he opposed systems of power that were dehumanizing. While his ministry included the 'least of these,' he also challenged the 'greatest of these' whenever humans were being treated as nonpersons."[49] This, along with worship of God, reclamation and liberation of the true concept of *imago Dei,* has become the African American church's *raison d'être* as subcommunity—a thinkable mode of ministry.

The Meaning of Empire

Despite America's unwillingness to see itself as an imperium in which the state wields power over individuals, the African American church (whose very existence is subcommunity) is the result and attestation of America as empire. In like judgment of John Dominic Crossan's necessary matrix for understanding early Christianity (i.e., Judaism within the Roman Empire),[50] African American presence within America is the necessary womb, not the annoying backdrop, against which to see America as empire and the African American church as subcommunity. Theft of people, exploitation, and despoliation of land are some of the obvious signs of America's earliest Roman-like empire activities. Despite some of the earlier signs of empiresque activity, the American people as a whole would rather not conceive of itself as such loathsome presence as that of empire. When asking "Why?" of the World Trade Centers and Pentagon attacks on

---

[49] J. Deotis Roberts, *The Prophethood of Black Believers: An African American Political Theology for Ministry* (Louisville, Kentucky: Westminster/John Knox Press, 1994), 2.

[50] John Dominic Crossan, *God and Empire: Jesus Against Rome, Then and Now* (HarperOne: Harper Collins Publisher, 2007), 1.

September 11, 2001, Americans seem to be suddenly awakened from sleep to recognize other countries' contempt of American imperialism. In Chalmers Johnson's seminal text, *The Sorrows of Empire*, Americans benightedly lamented, "Why do they hate us *so*? ...and the most common answer was 'jealousy.'"[51] The absurdity as to the cause for others' contempt or hatred of America was further proof of an imperial ideology[52] that had so permeated its core. It is vain to assert jealousy as the reason for contempt without any serious attempt to understand its origin. Professor James Cone stated once when addressing America's misapprehension of the African American community's hatred of America,

> The hate which black people feel toward whites is not due to the creation of the term "Black Power." Rather, it is a result of the deliberate and systematic ordering of society on the basis of racism, making black alienation not only possible but inevitable. For over three hundred years black people have been enslaved by the tentacles of American white power *empire* [emphasis mine], tentacles that worm their way into the guts of their being and "invade the gray cells of their cortex." For three hundred years they have cried, waited, voted, marched, picketed, and boycotted, but whites still refuse to recognize their humanity. In light of this, attributing black anger to the call for Black Power is ridiculous, if not obscene.[53]

Despite America's misapprehension concerning its place of hatred or contempt, Johnson said, "But a growing number finally began to grasp what most non-Americans already knew and had experienced over the previous half century—namely, that the United Sates was something other than what it professed to be, that it was, in fact, a

---

[51] Chalmers Johnson, *The Sorrows of Empire: Militarism, Secrecy, and the End of the Republic* (New York: Owl Book Henry Holt and Company, 2004), 4.

[52] John Dominic Crossan states that Rome's ideological power was created by Roman imperial theology, and it is not possible to overestimate its importance. Military power certainly secured the empire's external frontiers, but ideological power sustained its internal relations. Do not think of it as propaganda enforced by believing elites upon unbelieving masses. Think of it as persuasive advertising accepted very swiftly by all sides. As an American citizen I know too well of the prevalence of America's persuasive ideology of imperialism and purport that America is, as Crossan said, infected by such virus— imperialism.

[53] James H. Cone, *Black Theology and Black Power* (Maryknoll, New York: Orbis Books, 1997), 13.

military juggernaut intent on world domination."[54] Chalmers stated that, even after America comes to terms with its place as imperium, "Americans may still prefer to use *euphemisms* like 'lone superpower,' but since 9/11, our country has undergone a transformation from republic to empire that may well prove irreversible."[55] In *God and Empire*, Crossan asserts, "America is now—and may always have been—an empire and that, in fact, the virus of imperialism came—like so many others—on those first ships from Europe. The second and subsidiary claim is that America is Nova Roma, the New Roman Empire, Rome on the Potomac."[56] The empire that once ruled the world is now America—Nova Roma. Despite what America stated as a fledgling nation and what we believed about America as a republic, her earliest of ambitions were *absolutum dominium*—total and complete domination. As the Romans determined the conditions of Galilee,[57] Jesus' world, so too did the new Rome—America, Nova Roma[58]—determine and prescribe the terms and the conditions of the world of the African American.

Richard Horsley writes in *Jesus and Empire*, "The United States as the new Rome was from the beginning conceived as an empire, not just a republic."[59] In October 1492 Columbus began his intrusive exploration and expansion of the Americas by impinging upon the territory of native Americans. America's disregard for the civility and territory of others isn't a recent phenomenon; it began with Columbus' illegal search and seizure

---

[54]. Johnson, *The Sorrows of Empire*, 4.

[55] Ibid.

[56] Crossan, *God and Empire*, 2

[57] Horsley, *Jesus and Empire*, 15.

[58] Crossan, 2.

[59] Horsley, *Jesus and Empire*, 137.

of land occupied and owned by Native Indians. In a report back to the magistrate in Spain Columbus commented on the kindness of Native Indians, whom he would later take advantage of and exploit. "The Indians," Columbus reported, "are so naïve and so free with their possessions that no one who has not witnessed them would believe it. When you ask for something they have, they never say no. To the contrary, they offer to share with anyone."[60] America's barbarism/imperialism began with its blatant disregard of others, their territory and civility, and as such the African American church found itself strangely formed in America as empire.

As America formed itself nascently as an empire, Africans were its new subject people under Nova Roma—New Rome's empirical rule. As Norman Gottwald suggests,

> Empires, both ancient and modern, impose systems of domination parasitically on subject peoples. Empires, however, have taken different forms depending on historical circumstances. The major difference between ancient and modern empires is the mode of production.

Africans in the earliest stage of American imperialism were its sole labor force as they suffered unduly under Nova Roma—the New Rome's—chattel system. Without any regard for slaves save their fitness for production the New Rome and New Caesar forced them to work from "sunup to sundown"[61] in harvesting and producing goods for Nova Roma—the new Roman empire. Commenting on the cruelty, savagery, and barbarity of slavery, Hopkins shares an account of an ex-slave,

> Our labour was extremely hard, being obliged to work in the summer from about two o'clock in the morning, till about ten or eleven o'clock at night, and in the winter from four in the morning, till ten at night. The horses usually rested about

---

[60] Ibid, 3.

[61] Hopkins, *Down, Up, and Over*, 51.

five hours in the day, while we were at work; thus did the beasts enjoy greater privileges than we did.[62]

Obsessed with expansion, domination, production, and harvesting of crops, the new Roman empire had no human regard for slaves' lives. Millions of Africans were taken from their homes, land, and structures to which they were accustomed. They were now in an unfamiliar territory and system of a new world/empire that was totally foreign to them, and they struggled to make meaning of it. According to Albert J. Raboteau, church historian, "When Africans were brought into slavery, they were not merely transported from one world to another—one culture to another—but rather they and their humanity were transformed. They were torn away from structures and systems that had ordered their lives."[63] They had become something other than what and who God had created.

In addressing the systemic causes and absurdities of racism, racial hierarchy, skin privilege and white supremacy, Dwight Hopkins addressed the heart of such issues and treatment of Africans/blacks:

> Coupled with the realization that there is nothing divine about the racial hierarchy in the United States, we have to grasp the initial point of creation. God created all of humanity to live in harmony. The end goal, the *telos*, likewise draws all humanity toward harmonious living. Yet, the evil of white supremacy has subverted both sacred creation and holy goals. Whites with power redefined black as evil. Hoarding communal resources as monopolized private property, powerful white families defied divine creation and its *telos* and crafted one of the most sinister racial asymmetries in human history.[64]

---

[62] Ibid.

[63] Stacey Floyd-Thomas, et al., *Black Church Studies: An Introduction* (Nashville: Abingdon Press, 2001), 122.

[64] Eleazar S. Fernandez and Fernando F. Segovia, *A Dream Unfinished* (Maryknoll, New York: Orbis Books, 2001), 76.

Despite the horrors of chattel slavery—an Americanized and most egregious form—Hopkins also noticed the resilience and unfettered hope of the slaves under the rule of this new world/empire,

> Black people in America *as empire* [emphasis mine] have survived and thrived with a spirit of hope and determination. Even with 100 million of their African ancestors stolen from the Continent, 246 years of slavery, 100 years of legal segregation, and decades of de facto oppression, something has kept them on a path toward freedom. A way of holding on to this something has been passed down from generation to generation.[65]

The hope and way of holding on to which Hopkins refers is constitutive to the African American church and its lived experience. Hopkins quotes Professor James Evans as saying that, amid the horrid realities of slavery and the middle passage, the people of the African American church "have been believers." Such hope and belief has provided the African American church with a voice and a position from which to counter claims of imperialism and activities that resemble empire. In its varied forms, the appearances of empire are to be noted and countered as God created all men to be free.

Believing itself to have a special relationship with the Bible, while at the same time imitating the identity of Rome America was destined as an empire.[66] Richard Horsley states,

> Lest we think that the Bush-Cheney administration's invasion and occupation of Iraq is a sudden departure from a previously nonimperial American stance, we should check our American history books. The Bush administration's rationale for aggressive military action in the Middle East strongly resembles what American preachers as well as presidents were saying a century ago during the high point of American imperial ideology. And American identity as the New Rome goes back at least to the founding generations of Jefferson and Madison.

---

[65] Dwight N. Hopkins, *Introducing Black Theology of Liberation*, 1.

[66] Richard A. Horsley, ed., *In the Shadow of Empire: Reclaiming the Bible as a History of Faithful Resistance* (Louisville: Westminster John Knox Press, 2008), 1.

The latter understood themselves to be establishing a republic, in imitation of ancient Rome.[67]

In some way America's actions were sanctioned by God—the God of the Bible and the god of empire as she continued her barbarity and inhumane treatment of other people of God, primarily Africans and Native Americans. Commenting on the way in which America viewed itself in relation to the Bible and its imagery Horsley stated,

> Most Americans think of themselves as biblical people. From the very beginning Americans have thought of themselves as God's New Israel. The Pilgrims and Puritans and others who settled in New England were embarking on a new exodus to escape the pharaoh-like tyranny of English monarchs. The Mayflower Compact and scores of town charters created new covenant communities in which not only the congregational church but civil governments were patterned after Israel's covenant with God on Sinai and Jesus' Sermon on the Mount.[68]

According to John Dominic Crossan, it was necessary for America or any empire to believe *theologically* in its establishment to secure and assert its transcendence and sovereignty as a state.[69] Such belief, along with the presence of coins, structures, and images/*flags,* was the imperial glue[70] and reminder of the ubiquity of empire and imperial rule. Impassioned with zeal, religious or otherwise, America set out to establish itself as an empire.[71] Upon examination of the zeal and passion of the West, Randall Robinson quotes William Woodruff in his novel, *Quitting America*:

> No civilization prior to the European had occasion to believe in the systematic material progress of the whole human race; no civilization placed such stress upon the quantity rather than the quality of life; no civilization drove itself so

---

[67] Ibid., 3.

[68] Ibid.

[69] Crossan, *God and Empire*, 15.

[70] Ibid.

[71] Randall Robinson, *Quitting America* (New York: Dutton, 2004), 36.

> relentlessly to an ever-receding goal; no civilization was so passion-charged to replace what is with what could be; no civilization had striven as the West had done to direct the world according to its will; no civilization has known so few moments of peace and tranquility.[72]

Robinson noticed the absence of extremes and limits to which the west would not go in its pursuit of imperial domination and rule. The West seemed to be obsessed with establishing itself as a mega/superpower. Despite the West's practices of imperialism, the African American church functioned as the social and political consciousness in the black community, preaching an emancipatory gospel of liberation and reclamation. Even while in slavery, the African American church that was birthed in the hush harbors amid America as empire knew the absolute rule and authority of God and spoke incessantly of the justice of God. The justice which they advocated was necessary as they endured ills of Americanized slavery.

The African American church has long been the locus for preaching, but it has also been the meeting place of movements that countered the claims of imperialism and empire. The civil rights movements of the 60s were started and supported often by churches within the black communities. The African American church in American imperialism met regularly to pray for the success of nonviolent resistance movements and the justice of God while simultaneously praying for the fall of empire/systems that did not offer themselves for the good of humankind and precisely the black community.

America as empire has always been viewed askance by the one institution—the black church. The African American church in its regalia viewed itself too as the new Israel, not in terms of supersessionism or new people of God but the people of God through whom

---

[72] Ibid.

He would do radical and new things. As ancient Israel was born as an anti-imperial movement which would break away from Egyptian and Babylonian domination and rule, i.e., empire,[73] the African American church too was formed as a liberation movement within the American empire. The African American church, along with other institutions and organizations affiliated with it within America as empire, organized and formed grassroots movements which countered American imperialism and its pervading injustice.

The benefit of such resistance and opposition to empire has yielded many of the progressive accomplishments and claims of the nation today, although it is still empire spewing imperial messages and isms. The influence and span of America as a nation does carry sway globally. However, the recent perception brought on by abuse of power has caused America as an empire to be loathed by many and has caused much social, civil, and intercultural unrest. As the African American church has been the forerunner in carrying the baton for social justice, it has not disinvited any one from joining in fighting against empire and its oppressive claims. America was born as a nation of diverse peoples, with some having secret and poisonous ambitions of hierarchical/imperial structure. The African American church understands, however, that opposing imperialism repairs community of its injuries caused by empire.

As a "balm in Gilead" the African American church since its beginnings has offered help, care, and ointments in the repair and healing of wounds. After receiving one of its members back from the lashings of an enraged master or official of the imperial order, the early black church would care for and comfort the afflicted. Even after one had

---

[73] Horsley, *In the Shadow of Empire*, 9.

been tragically separated from a mother or father or sibling in the savagery of empire, the black church would heal the brokenhearted. The black church in the effects of empire would still stretch forth its hand in the care and comfort of those who have been defrauded, cheated, and gypped by empire and its practices. Like the Messiah, who was wounded for our transgressions and bruised for our iniquities, the black church through its own brokenness/*wounds* offers healing to whosoever will—those wounded by empire—and by its stripes many have been and are healed.

The aim of Jesus' ministry was that while He sought to address the ills of empire, He also healed others of the harm and damage done by it. The gospels are accounts of instances wherein Jesus healed individuals and masses of the harm and injury of empire and its debilitating and oppressive rule. Jesus not only healed individually and en masse, He also sought to heal social bodies and structures that had enforced or re-enforced Roman imperialism. The method of Jesus' healing was not for the purpose of healing only, individually or even en masse. Jesus sought to heal and address structures, institutions, and social bodies co-opted by the triumphant imperialism of the Roman Empire.[74] Horsley argues,

> Like the exorcisms, Jesus' healings were not simply isolated acts of individual mercy, but part of a larger program of social as well as personal healing. The healing episodes in Mark's story that appear in sequences with sea crossings and wilderness feedings evoke memories of Moses and Elijah, the great founding and renewing prophets of Israel. In these healings and other "miracles," therefore, Mark's story represents Jesus as engaged in renewal of Israel—or of Israel plus other peoples, in that some of the incidents involve people in the villages beyond the frontiers of Galilee.[75]

---

[74] Ibid, 108.

[75] Ibid.

In the wake of anti-imperial resistance movements and the civil rights movement of the South, Jesus and the African American church continue to repair communities and institutions of the harmful and damaging effects of American imperialism

BIBLIOGRAPHY

Blount, Brian K. *Go Preach! Mark's Kingdom Message and the Black Church Today.* Maryknoll, New York: Orbis Books, 1998.

_____. *Then the Whisper Put on Flesh: New Testament Ethics in an African American Context.* Nashville: Abingdon Press, 2001.

Brueggemann, Walter. *A Commentary on Jeremiah: Exile and Homecoming.* Grand Rapids, Michigan: Eerdmans Publishing Company, 1998.

_____. *Texts That Linger, Words That Explode: Listening to Prophetic Voices.* Minneapolis: Fortress Press, 2000.

_____. *The Prophetic Imagination.* Minneapolis: Fortress Press, 2001.

_____. *The Word Militant: Preaching a Decentering Word.* Minneapolis: Fortress Press, 2007.

Cone, James H. *Black Theology and Black Power.* Maryknoll, New York: Orbis Books, 2001.

Crossan, John Dominic. *God and Empire: Jesus Against Rome, Then and Now.* New York: HarperOne, 2007.

Dixie, Quinton, Hosford, and Cornell West, eds. *The Courage to Hope: From Black Suffering to Human Redemption.* Boston: Beacon Press, 1999.

Fernandez, Eleazar S., and Fernando F. Segovia. *A Dream Unfinished.* Maryknoll, New York: Orbis Books, 2001.

Floyd-Thomas, Stacey, Juan Floyd-Thomas, Carol B. Duncan, Stephen G. Ray, Jr., and Nancy Lynne Westfield, *Black Church Studies: An Introduction.* Nashville: Abingdon Press, 2001.

Frazier, E. Franklin, and C. Eric Lincoln. *The Negro Church in America* and *The Black Church Since Frazier.* New York: Schocken Books, 1974.

Gafney, Wilda C. *Daughters of Miriam: Women Prophets in Ancient Israel.* Minneapolis: Fortress Press, 2008.

Herzog, William R. II. *Prophet and Teacher*. Louisville, Kentucky: Westminster John Knox Press, 2005.

Hogue, David A. *Remembering the Future, Imagining the Past: The Story, Ritual, and the Human Brain*. Eugene, Oregon: Wipf & Stock, 2003.

Hopkins, Dwight N. *Introducing Black Theology of Liberation*. Maryknoll, New York: Orbis Books, 1999.

_____. *Down, Up, and Over: Slave Religion and Black Theology*. Minneapolis: Fortress Press, 2000.

Horsley, Richard A., ed. *Jesus and Empire: The Kingdom of God and the New World Disorder*. Minneapolis: Fortress Press, 2003.

_____. *In the Shadow of Empire: Reclaiming the Bible as a History of Faithful Resistance*. Louisville: Westminster John Knox Press, 2008.

Howard, Gregory M. *Black Sacred Rhetoric: A Commentary for African-American Preaching*. South Carolina: Booksurge Publishing, 2008.

Johnson, Chalmers. *The Sorrows of Empire: Militarism, Secrecy, and the End of the Republic*. New York: Owl Book Henry Holt & Company, 2004.

Mitchell, Henry. *Black Church Beginnings: The Long-Hidden Realities of the First Years* Grand Rapids: Eerdmans Publishing Company, 2004.

Roberts, J. Deotis. *The Prophethood of Black Believers: An African American Political Theology for Ministry*. Louisville: Westminster John Knox Press, 1994.

Robinson, Randall. *Quitting America*. New York: Dutton, 2004.

Smith, Catherine Marie. *Preaching Justice: Ethnic and Cultural Perspectives*. Eugene, Oregon: Wipf & Stock, 1998.

A THEO-BIBLICAL CONTEXT FOR CONFRONTING THE ISSUES OF MARGINALIZATION ENDURED BY THE INCARCERATED
MATTHEW 25:31-46

Rev. Tyree A. Anderson, D.Min.

Biblical Context

In researching relevant quotations on the Bible, I discovered one that spoke clearly about justice, morality, and a faithful calling to accept the teachings of Jesus as noted in the Gospel accounts. Augustine of Hippo, the great African Father of the Church said, "If you believe what you like in the Gospel, and reject what you don't like, it is not the Gospel you believe, but yourself" (Paine 2013, Veracity). This quote is a reminder that all who read its hallowed words that justice must remain on the table if the kingdom of God is to be established. Specifically, the Gospel reminds us that incarcerated and imprisoned individuals must never be forgotten or ignored. There is a distinctive difference between incarceration and imprisonment. Imprisonment means to be in a confined space in reference to a jail or prison. Incarceration is different and more systemic. Incarceration does not occur when a person finally arrives in prison. I contend that incarceration begins when a person born into a particular situation where physical degradation, economic exploitation, cultural appropriation, and political dislocation has occurred (Anderson, 2016, 1). Incarceration is that state of being where a person is born into a confined environment of political, educational, economic, and social disadvantage. Further, these significant components contribute to the creation of psychological, emotional, mental, and even spiritual constructs of the human condition leading to the behaviors considered as criminal in nature by the society that created the conditions that ultimately escorts a person into imprisonment (Anderson, 2016, xi).

The incarcerated are living in the margins and they typically come from communities that are marginalized economically, politically, and socially. Jesus identifies with the forgotten and ignored; therefore, what is done to these is as much done to Jesus. The biblical text is clear on the expectant role of the church for those Jesus categorizes as the "least of these" (Matt. 25:31-46). The church--in this case, the Black Church--is to have a heart for and provide ministry to those that society has deemed as unredeemable.

Matthew 25:31-46 is the passage of scripture that I have chosen for this project in discovering the attitudes of members concerning the development of incarceration ministries in the Black Church (see Clarks chapter). This particular pericope challenges disciples of Jesus from Nazareth to be involved in matters of social justice, specifically to minister and remember those who are both incarcerated and in prison.

This passage offers a unique opportunity for those who declare their fellowship and faith in Jesus to demonstrate it by serving those who are perpetually connected to the criminal justice system. Moreover, this passage challenges the Black Church and its leaders to be concerned about more than salvation. The Black Church must evolve beyond the traditional (i.e., classical) readings of the passage and be progressive in its approach. However, the traditional approach appears to be more comfortable.

The traditional approach can be seen in the works of Boring (1994), Keener (1999), and Morris (1992). Boring proposes that this pericope was "not a parable, but an apocalyptic drama" that unfolds in the final judgment of humanity as the "coming of the Son of Man with his angels" assembles "all nations before his throne—and modulates into affirmations of the ultimate importance of ordinary, this-worldly deeds" (Boring 1994, 455). Furthermore, Boring proposes that two kingdoms stand in opposition to each other. The Son of Man who sits on the throne to judge individuals and nations represents one kingdom; and the other kingdom stands to be judged by the Son of Man for its actions toward those whom the Son of Man considers members of his family. Boring notes that "the kingdom of God is disclosed as the only true kingdom" and that it is evident by the service it offers to those identified as the "least of these" (Boring 1994, 244). The word rendered service, also means to minister; which Boring states is "the final summary of deeds performed by the righteous and neglected by the condemned" (Boring 1994, 245).

The idea of the righteous and the condemned is identified by Keener as the sheep and the goats. Keener, unlike Boring identifies the genre of this passage as a parable. He comments that the passage "assumes a high Christology" and uses the parabolic form "the Son of Man" to establish the authenticity of the passage (Keener 1999, 602). Furthermore, the language of the text, (i.e., sheep, goats, and siblings) contains parable-like characteristics. Keener differs from the dispensational explanations of Boring and submits that the passage is instead concerned with how the nations "responded to the Gospel of the kingdom already preached to them before the time of his kingdom" (Keener 1999, 605). To do ministry in this context means to not just hear the message about the kingdom, but to do what the message instructs, i.e., feed the hungry, quench those that thirst, welcome strangers, clothe the naked, care for the sick, and visit the imprisoned.

Morris' interpretation, similar to Keener, is concerned with the accountability of individuals who hear the Gospel message. In examining the passage, Morris stated, "it puts strong emphasis on the truth that ultimately every person on earth will be called upon to account for his or her use of the opportunities of service experienced through life" (Morris 1992, 633). For Morris, faith and grace are secondary to works as evidence of salvation. Works or the lack thereof according to Morris serve as the "evidence either of the grace of God…or the rejection of that grace" (Morris 1992, 633). Therefore, salvation is tied to the service one offers toward those living in the margins.

It is from the margins that ministry becomes the most relevant. This is not to discount the possibility of ministry being offered in the marketplace, but there is a definitive difference between ministry in the margins and ministry in the marketplace. It is customary to find those who operate in the marketplace upholding the traditional approach.

A marketplace reading of the text allows those who are in power to maintain the status quo. However, those who read the same passage from the margins as those who are in the marketplace will often come to contradictory interpretations that invoke them to speak truth to power. The Black Church cannot afford to read the Bible through a marketplace lens if it is to be transformative for the incarcerated and imprisoned.

To see Jesus outside of the margins is to essentially miss Jesus altogether. The Jesus of the Bible has more in common with people living in the margins than those who are in the marketplace. In his book *Jesus and the Disinherited*, Howard Thurman reminds us to examine Jesus within His context. Thurman notes, "We begin with the simple historical fact that Jesus was a Jew. The second important fact is that Jesus was a poor Jew. The third fact is that Jesus was a member of a minority group in the midst of a larger dominant and controlling group" (Thurman 1976, 15-18).

The facts established by Thurman are found within the Gospel writings themselves. From the prologue in the Gospel According to Matthew to the Calvary experience, Jesus identifies with those who were oppressed politically and religiously. Jesus, according to Thurman was also poor. In the Gospel According to Luke, there is a well-detailed story that Jesus' mother and earthly father were poor. The Gospel writer Luke notes that when Jesus was dedicated at the temple, Mary and Joseph made the sacrifice "according to that which is said in the law of the Lord, A pair of turtledoves, or two young pigeons" (Luke 2:24). Furthermore, Thurman argues that Jesus was a member of an oppressed group living within the confines of a dominant group. This assessment aligns with what William H. Myers, notes in "Jesus Christ and the Poor: The Bible, the Poor, and the Black Church." Jesus was poor and in being poor, Myers points out that the "Hebrew terms for 'poor' can stand for the materially needy, the socially oppressed, or spiritually lowly" (Myers 2007, 1581 a-g). Using Luke's story of worldwide accountability (taxation and a census count) imposed upon all who were under the imperial influence of Rome. The chronicling of the oppressive powers notes that in the Gospel accounts Jesus never identified himself with the rich and powerful, but those who live in the margins.

The evidence in the Gospels is overwhelming that Jesus of Nazareth was in fact a member of a poor marginalized community and that He rose from the bowels of a voiceless existence to call to task those who purposely misused the Torah for their own selfish purposes. Jesus, according to Myers, had a heart that was "directed toward the people whose fate in life gave them no other recourse than to accept a lowly and meaningless way of living, these were the people who had to succumb to those unavoidable circumstances that prevailed over their personal lives" (Myers 2007, 1581 a-g). The images that portray a Jesus that is meek and lowly are widely accepted, but this is not the Jesus found in the biblical narrative. The Jesus in the Gospels is less concerned about saving souls and going to heaven than he is about building up those who are victims of imperial and religious power. He accomplished this by confronting those who were devaluing, and even in many cases destroying those who were perpetual victims of imperial powers. This view is more advanced than the traditional one that only examines Jesus from a soul salvation perspective.

New Testament and Matthew scholar, Warren Carter offers a non-traditional perspective where he applies a sociopolitical approach to the text. Carter's concern is the marginalized and not the powerful. The powerful will be judged because they have oppressed the poor and purposely disenfranchised them. Furthermore, "judgment follows the opportunity that all have to respond to the disciples' proclamation" (Carter 2000, 492).

Jesus, in Carter's context is the Son of Man, who calls for a commitment to minister to the poor. Viewing this passage through an eschatological lens can motivate us to remember those who are often last in every social category. Carter argues that this passage (Matt. 25:31-46) further establishes a final judgment to come from the Son of Man. He states, "Standard features include the majestic judge, angels, the assembling of the people to be judged, the separation, the reward of the righteous and punishment of the wicked, the establishment of God's empire," (Carter 2000, 491). Carter's view on the Son of Man connects to that of W.F. Albright and C.S. Mann.

Albright and Mann offer an insight into the title that Jesus often referred to himself as, Son of Man (speaking in a third person context). The Son of Man, according to Albright and Mann is expanded in Matthew over that which is found in the Gospel of Mark. In Matthew, Jesus as the Son of Man has primarily two main functions. First, the Son of Man counters the kingdom of evil by preaching and teaching about the kingdom of God, which brings men, women, boys, and girls from darkness into the light. Secondly, the Son of Man is the judge of all and the final authority on all things. The Son of Man is viewed through an eschatological lens (Albright and Mann 1971, lxxxiii-lxxxix). It is through this lens that the Son of Man in Matthew 25:31-46, finally establishes himself as the mighty magistrate who will ensure that divine justice is carried out to rebalance the scales of life. For Albright and Mann, the Son of Man is unlike any other judge, because he resonates and identifies himself with those who are marginalized and mistreated by the kingdom of men (Albright and Mann 1971, 303-310).

As the Son of Man, Jesus demonstrates to the marginalized that one does not have to sit idly by and be a victim of oppression and systematic extermination. Within each individual and within each community victims of oppression can resist the powers that are designed to destroy any hope of meaningful existence. Charles L. Campbell outlines this position in his book, *The*

Word Before the Powers (2002). Campbell, in using language developed by Walter Wink, identified imperial powers as a Domination System. Campbell points out that Jesus' ministry is one of resistance to temptation. Campbell notes, "His ministry will be one of resistance to the principalities and powers of the world. In addition, Jesus' temptation is inescapably linked to his crucifixion, highlighting the fact that Jesus' ministry of resistance leads to his execution by the powers" (Campbell 2002, 45).

Moreover, in Matthew 25:31-46, Jesus identifies with what many would consider to be the lowest members of society. This pericope is considered by many to be a judgment on the nations. In these particular verses, Jesus not only identifies with "the least of these," Jesus is blatantly clear when He distinguishes them as part of His family. Matthew paints this picture of Jesus coming as the Son of Man to sit as a king to judge nations on their treatment of the poor, imprisoned, naked, homeless, and forgotten. This is a reflection of individuals and their spirituality, as well as a reflection of their political position in society.

In his book, the *Politics of Jesus*, Obery M. Hendricks Jr. notes that, "According to the politics of Jesus, those in positions of leadership, secular, or religious, who are self-important and always seeking self-aggrandizement are not worthy to lead people, because they do not treat the people's needs as holy," (Hendricks 2006, 177). The needs of the people that Jesus identifies with have been largely ignored by society. What has not been ignored is the political support for major transnational and national corporations that establish business pursuits--often at the expense of human lives and communities. America has been home to two major life-altering agencies. The first was chattel slavery and the second, the prison industrial complex. Both were created to make a profit and both have attempted to become rooted in a biblical foundation. However, neither of these industries can be supported using the biblical text. This is the perspective of Raymond E. Brown.

Because the majority of inmates in prison are Black, it requires a fresh reading of the passage to ensure that cultural distinctions are considered before making any form of application. Brown, much like W.E.B. Dubois, identifies that Jesus defines the poor as not just financially impoverished, but those who were "maimed, lame, blind" and those who were victims of the powerful (Brown 2007, 91). This typically defines the plight of Black Americans. The impoverished are the perpetual victims of the rich and powerful. Although Brown does not mention the incarcerated, they clearly fall into the category of the poor and impoverished, i.e., the least of these.

Jesus reminded those given positions of power that they would be held responsible for their actions toward the poor and oppressed. Instead of remaining indifferent towards the lack of justice for the dispossessed, Jesus constantly stood up and prophetically pronounced judgment on the hypocritical system and its engineers who refused to enact *misphat* on behalf of the dispossessed of society. Hendricks supports this argument. In his book *The Politics of Jesus,* argues that salvation and condemnation will not be measured by, "religious practice, or memorization of scripture, or even faithful attendance at church or temple" (Hendricks 2006, 9). Instead, all will be judged on "whether we have tried to relieve the plight of the hungry and dispossessed and those stripped of their freedom; whether we have tried to change this war-torn world to a world free from oppression and exploitation, so that all of God's children might have life and that more abundantly" (Hendricks 2006, 9). Hendricks further stresses his point by noting that, "Jesus identified so completely with the oppressed that he made an astonishing declaration that today's political leaders—religious leaders, too—would do well to remember: ' as you have not done it to the least of these, you have not done it to me'" (Hendricks 2006, 9).

The incarcerated are living in the margins. This marginalization extends to their home communities economically, politically, and socially. The non-traditional view of "the least of these," as those who are vulnerable and marginalized identified through a non-traditional perspective, offers those rooted in a liberation mindset a needed understanding of the requirement of those called to minister to the marginalized as well as the incarcerated and imprisoned.

Theological Context

The problem facing the Black Church and the Black community is more than an uncritical exegesis of the biblical text as it pertains to the incarcerated, but also in how God is understood and related to on a daily basis. In other words, how the Black Church chooses to define God and the role of God in the life of the Black religious experience will determine how the Black Church will address the issue of incarceration. The theology of the Black Church must move beyond the salvation of the soul and invest in discovering how best to address the plight of the people. The Black Church must have a theology that speaks to and challenges the current power structure that continues to benefit from the system of incarceration. In order to begin a new approach to bring awareness to the Black Church and eventually dismantle systemic issues with incarceration, I believe the Black Church must be a location where hope and restoration are offered.

The theological foundation for my project is grounded in a Black Liberation Theology and Anthropology. They inform my project because of the experience, history, and cultural disregard White supremacy and its system of domination have toward the Black body. Black Theological Anthropology as identified by Dwight Hopkins in his book *Being Human: Race Culture and Religion* (2005) speaks to the humanity of people who are made in the image of God, and who are the victims of oppression and proposes alternatives for the marginalized in society. Theologian, James Cone who is considered the father of Black Theology identifies the six sources of Black Theology that inform the Black consciousness. Those six sources described by Cone are Black Experience, Black History, Black Culture, Revelation, Scripture, and Tradition. For purposes of my project, I will focus on the following three, Black Experience, Black History, and Black Culture (Cone 2005, 23-35).

The Black Experience must be understood through Black religion, namely the Black Church. The genius of the Black Church and its authority is rooted in the hermeneutical application of the biblical text. To say it another way, the Black Church experience cannot be experienced without the sacred text known as the Bible.

In *Black Church Studies: An Introduction*, the authors note that the Bible is, "a guidebook to an appropriation of the Bible as a historical narrative of its own contemporary experience" (Floyd-Thomas et al.. 2007, 51). The Bible is revered as sacred but can reveal the secular. In other words, the correlation of the Black experience and Black spirituality can be understood in the stories of the Bible. This is best understood through the stories of the Exodus event and the Jesus story.

Black people who arrived in America as slaves found it necessary to enter into a mode of survival. The Exodus event and the Jesus story serve as the foundation of the Black Church's belief system. These stories are paramount to living, and these stories helped remind them that though they were slaves, God had the power to free them and transform their situation. God used two leaders in the biblical narrative, Moses and Jesus, to defy the status quo and challenge the political power that oppressed the people. The Moses and Exodus event retained its purpose in the minds of Black people who experienced inequality and found a kindred relationship with those who were slaves like them. The death of Pharaoh and the miracle of walking on dry land gave them hope that God would raise up a leader like Moses to deliver them from the harsh reality of chattel slavery. However, the most important person in the faith of Black people in the Black church is Jesus of Nazareth.

Jesus' life was characterized by oppression and poverty, very much like the slave. However, in spite of all the hurdles to personhood in first century Palestine, Jesus rose to challenge those who purposely denied the rights afforded to those who are children of God. Frequently, Jesus, like tax collectors, prostitutes, and alcoholics was not welcomed in the temple or valued in society. This describes the Black experience. It is for this reason that Jesus is loved by Black people. Their experiences are identical. Jesus chose to identify himself with the rejected of society. Black people readily identified with Him, because in America, historically, the dejected and social outcast in society is anyone who had the characteristics and features of their African ancestors. The Blacks in America have always been the "other" and Jesus identified himself as a family member of the "other."

No one feels discarded more than the incarcerated. The incarcerated feel trapped on every side and there appears to be no hope in sight, because the modern rendition of the Black Church has failed to live up to its historical identity. I believe the Black Church has been and, at least for the foreseeable future, will continue to be the most complex organism that exists between heaven and earth. In this age of incarceration, the Black Church must provide practical tools and methods that go beyond religious and cultural survival. It must provide guidance, hope, and stability for the Black community and those who are suffering from incarceration. Furthermore, the Black church must be able to cast a vision that articulates and demonstrates aspects of liberation to those whom it has been called to serve. In other words, the Black church must go beyond the rhetoric of liberation actually to perform the ethic of liberation. The Black experience demands that the Black church remain sacred while confronting the secular. Furthermore, the Black Church must adopt a *sankofa* perspective to capitalize on its historical value.

In using Black Theological Anthropology, the importance of history must be included while the Black Church moves forward. Theological Anthropology is vital because it helps to position a person or people within the proper historical timeframe and theological reference so life-transforming work can occur. "The fundamental nature of Theological Anthropology within Black Church theology is twofold in that it restores and sustains the humanity of Black persons in the face of cultural and religious discourses that would deny this recognition. This nature is grounded in the divine-human relationship" (Floyd-Thomas et al. 2007, 51). In other words, one cannot begin to address the restoration of a people without first confronting systemic evils that work tirelessly using religious language to justify various levels of oppression.

The human condition in discussion is incarceration in general, and more specifically, the incarceration of Black bodies in a historical context that dates to a time where American chattel slavery was the norm (Slave era). Beyond being the norm, it was a theological reality justified by proponents of White supremacy. The one institution that became the voice for the voiceless and hope for the hopeless in a White supremacy dominated culture was the Black Church.

In *God of the Oppressed,* James Cone describes his love for the Black Church, and its importance to him as a child growing up in Bearden, Arkansas. Cone states,

> The black Church taught me how to deal with the contradictions of life and provided a way to create meaning in a society not of my own making. In the larger 'secular' black community, this perspective on life is often called the 'art of survival'; but in the black Church, we call it the 'grace of God.' It is called survival because it is a way of remaining physically alive in a situation of oppression without losing one's dignity. We call it grace because we know it to be an unearned gift from God who is the giver of 'every good and perfect gift'. (Cone 1975, 2)

The Black Church gave dignity to a group of people discarded by society. It is this same dignity that must be extended to those who are incarcerated and imprisoned. Hope is restored in life through this dignity. I believe that the Black Church is still the most important institution in the Black community. From the pulpits to its choir lofts, the message of hope from the Black Church still rings loud and true for anyone who is desolate.

The quintessential ingredient that transforms a life from despair, dejection, and despondency to one that is full of joy, peace, and unlimited potential is hope. Hope is rooted in a theology that says, "God has not forgotten me." Those who are marginalized must have a theology rooted in hope. Hope originates from God, but is administered by the church. Cone proposes that, the role of the church is threefold: first it proclaims the reality of divine liberation; second it actively shares in the liberation struggle; third the church as a fellowship is a visible manifestation that the Gospel is a reality (Cone 2005, 130-132). He further states accurately that, "if the church is not free, if it is a distorted representation of the irruption of God's kingdom, if it lives according to the old order (as it usually has), then no one will believe its message" (Cone 2005, 131-132).

The role of the Black church has never been more direr than now. When incarceration and imprisonment rates are skyrocketing, unemployment numbers are extreme, and violence in poor communities is catastrophic, I contend that something must be done. I believe that it is time for the Black church to assume the position it has held for years—leader of the people and this nation. It is not the role of the politician to declare hope and change, but for the prophetic preacher to proclaim a message hope to the hopeless.

Hope begins in the house of God, not in the legislative halls of government. This is why the Black church must take an active role in ministering to the margins and using Anthropology rooted in Black Theology as the grounds for change. Those who are incarcerated and imprisoned that hear the message of hope are able to redefine themselves despite their past.

The plight of the incarcerated is not up for pontificating or for talking heads to engage in frivolous debates. The time for talking is over because real people, with real problems, often times have no real solutions to help them overcome their incarcerated context. These incarcerated individuals are often never allowed to define who they are, nor are they able to reinvent themselves to reach their full potential. Their experiences within the context of White supremacy demand that someone speak into their lives to offer them hope, regardless of their current contextual situation. There is a great need for them to recognize their humanity in the face of oppression that purposely denies their personhood.

Liberation theologian, Gustavo Gutierrez proposes that God favors the poor (1973, 1984). In the essay, *Marginalized People, Liberating Perspectives: A Womanist Approach to Biblical Interpretation*, Kelly Brown Douglas points out that Gutierrez suggested, "there is a 'preferential option for the poor.' That is to say, the revelation of God is best understood from the vantage point of the marginalized, the oppressed, the least of these in society" (Brown Douglas 2001, 41-47). Therefore, there is a need for a new vision, new voice; and where those who are incarcerated are often times hopeless. A new culture must rise from the ashes like a phoenix and the catalyst must be the Black Church. Dwight Hopkins proposes such a change begins with how we view our theological anthropology.

In *Being Human: Race, Culture, and Religion*, Dwight Hopkins notes, "theological anthropology grows out of culture; culture arises from particular selves and the self; and selves/self automatically involve the race of the selves/self who create cultures out of which we construct contemporary theological anthropology," (Hopkins 2005, 4). In other words, the community (sacred and human relationships) takes precedence over the individual in helping to reestablish a culture of inclusion, dignity, and hope. In what is a justifiable critique of the dominant American culture, i.e. individualism, Hopkins establishes the dangers of how individualism stands against the fabric of community as taught by Jesus and those who are avid disciples of his teaching.

> The U.S.A.'s implicit yet dominant theological anthropology is demonic individualism. The demon reveals itself in a kind of American cultural trinity: (1) historical amnesia, (2) instantaneous fulfillment of desire, and (3) 'we're number one' mythology. All three contribute to a rabid individualism that amounts to a rival religion or idolatrous notion of the self, the community, and the divine. (Hopkins 2005 4-5)

This culture stands against justice (justice not only for the individual, but also for the community) and it is blind to the needs of those who are incarcerated and imprisoned.

In the essay, *(De)Constructing Justice,* Tony Jones points out that one of the main concerns on God's agenda for the Israelites before they entered the Promised Land was how the stranger was treated. For followers of Jesus, justice is not something to discuss, but something that must be done. Jones notes,

> The passion for justice among Christ-followers, of course, is more than some ethereal 'sense.' Instead, it's based on a text and a history that give us some very completing examples of what justice is…With a hermeneutic of humility, Christians are less apt to spend their time writing books on apologetics and more likely to link arms with those with whom they disagree (even those from other religions) and fight for justice. (Jones 2009, 59-63)

What Jones says applies to those who are incarcerated. Often, the incarcerated have become perpetual victims of those who engage in what Hopkins identifies as "rabid individualism," that will not bring justice or healing to a community, but further divides it along a capitalistic structure.

Black Theological Anthropology has a cultural aspect to it, and manifests itself in how Black people choose to carry out a faith rooted in a God who chose to reveal Godself in the person of Jesus Christ. In other words, the faith of Black people as carried out in the Black Church rests on a belief in a God that sits high and looks low. The faith is in a liberation-minded God who delivered the Children of Israel from Egyptian bondage. Additionally, the faith is rooted in a belief that the love of God is so great, that God would become human to live and experience what it means to be oppressed, while introducing the idea that within the oppressed exists a kingdom to which there is no end (*Being Human*). The Black Church operating in a Black Theological Anthropology construct will never replicate a White supremacy version of Christ, but will instead embody "The Black Christ," as described by Kelly Brown Douglas.

Brown Douglas offers to the marginalized and incarcerated Black person a new vision of Christ that has been rescued from the classical Europeanized rendition of Christ. The European version of Christ has been the face of White supremacy for Black people since 1619. The Black Church continued to promote a White image of divinity, which came under attack by Black clergy and scholars who challenged the very image of "Christ" that had been promoted since the Renaissance Era. It is interesting that the synonym for the word renaissance is rebirth, revival, and regeneration; none of which has happened on a large scale to liberate the Black Church from the overbearing cultural influences of Western Civilization (*The Black Christ*).

What Brown Douglas does in looking at the theological justification of a Black Christ is to rebut the belief in a White Christ, who undergirds White supremacy. In support of his case that Jesus' experience was Black, James Cone uses Albert Cleage's argument that proposes that Jesus was ethnically Black because of his relationship with the oppressed, i.e. Black people (Cone 1970, 38). James J. Gardiner and J. Deotis Roberts saw Christ's universality with all of humanity, which rescues Jesus from being White only (*The Quest for Black Theology*). Brown Douglas helps us to see that there was a concerted effort being waged to confront White supremacy (Brown Douglas 1994, 53-64).

The image of a Black Christ from a cultural perspective does more to transform a Black community than any form of legislation. With that said, I contend that the Black Church must be involved in the cultural shaping of its congregation and its involvement with those who are incarcerated. For if Jesus, who identifies with the "least of these," is Black, then the embodiment of Christ lived in an incarcerated environment controlled by the Romans, i.e. White supremacy. Therefore, it is incumbent upon the Black Church to be intimately involved in cultural formation of its community. The identity and theological message must be properly readdressed.

I believe that the message of a Black Christ has been lost and even distorted because the Black Church as a collective refuses to address racial disparities or because it wants to avoid being blamed for using the race card. However, for those living outside the margins and incarcerated due to political and economic realities, they must hear sermons and messages that connect their incarcerated situation with one who intimately relates to their situation, i.e., Black Christ.

The need for a prophetic voice to address incarceration is required today. In her essay, *Ethics as an Art Doing the Work Our Souls Must Have*, Emilie M. Townes points out six key threads of a prophetic voice. Although written from a Womanist perspective, her analysis applies to those who are victims of an incarceration-focused society. The six threads are:

1) The desire and the ability to discern the will of God
2) The prophetic also exposes the oppressive nature of society.
3) The prophetic voice must be an agent of admonition.
4) A womanist ethic is unapologetically confrontive.
5) The prophetic voice seeks to create a community of faith, partnership, justice, and unity.
6) The prophetic voice recognizes that self-critical inclusivity is mandatory. (Townes 2011, 43-47)

When considering the plight of the incarcerated, I believe Townes' six threads directly correlate to the expected role of the Black pastor and pulpit in confronting purposely-oppressive systems. Therefore, messages that remove the otherworldly aspects of salvation and brings the

Christ back into focus where His humanity is on full display is needed to address incarceration. What it does is brings humanity into the forefront of all spiritual discussions.

This draws us back to Hopkins who informs us that, "one becomes a human being by gearing all ultimate issues toward compassion for and empowerment of people in structural poverty, working-class folk, and the marginalized" (Hopkins 2005, 7). This is the Black Christ and it is this message that offers hope; and within the Black Church, hope is an ever-pressing point.

A theological perspective to address issues of incarceration and even imprisonment must go beyond the traditional salvific theology; it must be rooted in a practical aspect that addresses the root causes of the problems. The Black Church must engage individuals and systems, which foster conditions that breed environments for incarceration. I believe this is possible when the Black Church uses a theology not rooted in White supremacy. Instead, it is my belief that the Black Church must implement a Black Theological Anthropology strategy that focuses on Mission and Hope (*Being Human* and *Reimagining the Human*). The reason being is that a Black Theological Anthropology of Mission and Hope sits at the heart of the Black experience, is rooted in Black history, and is the basis for a Black culture that can challenge outdated theological presuppositions that justify the exploitation and occupation of a people viewed as unredeemable.

BIBLIOGRAPHY

Anderson, Tyree Antonio. 2016. "A Project to Discover Attitudes on Incarceration at the Bethel Batpist Church, Tallahassee, Florida." (Accessed September 2019)

Brown, Michael Joseph. 2007. *The Gospel of Matthew - True to Our Native Land: An African Ameican New Testatment Commentary.* Edited by Brian K. Blount. Minneapolis: Fortress Press

Campbell, Charles L. 2002. *The Word Before the Powers: An Ethic of Preaching.* Louisville: Westminister John Knox Press.

Carter, Warren. 2000. *Matthew and the Margins.* Maryknoll: Orbis Books

Cone, James H. 2005. *A Black Theology of Liberation: Twentieth Anniversary Edition.* Maryknoll: Orbis Books.

_____. 1975. *God of the Oppresed.* New York: Seabury Press.

_____. 2012 *The Cross and the Lynching Tree.* Maryknoll: Orbis Books.

Douglas, Kelly Brown. 1994. *The Black Christ.* Maryknoll: Orbis Books.

Floyd-Thomas, Stacey, Juan Floyd-Thomas, Carol B. Duncan, Stephen G. Ray Jr., and Nancy Lynne Westfield. 2007. *Black Church Studies: An Introduction.* Nashville: Abingdon Press.

Gutierrez, Gustavo. 1973. *A Theology of Liberation.* Maryknoll: Orbis.

Hendricks, Obery M. Jr.2006. *The Politics of Jesus: Rediscovering the True Revolutionary Nature of Jesus' Teachings and How They Have Been Corrupted.* New York: Random House.

Hopkins, Dwight. 2005. *Being Human: Race, Culture, and Religion.* Minneapolis: Fortress Press.

Ironside, H.A. 2005. *Matthew.* Grand Rapids, MI: Kregal Publications.

Jones, Tony. 2009. "(De)constructing Justice: What does the Post Modern Turn Contribute to the Christian Passion for Justice." *In The Justice Project*, edited by Brian McLaren, Elisa Padilla, and Ashley Bunting Seeber, 58-63. Grand Rapids: Baker Books.

Keener, Craig S. 1999. *A Commentary on the Gospel of Matthew.* Grand Rapids: Wm. B. Eerdmans Co.

Mann, W.F., Albright C.S. 1971. *Matthew.* New Haven, CT: Yale University Press.

Morris, Leon. 1992. *The Gospel According to Matthew.* Grand Rapids: Wm. B. Eerdmans Publishing Co.

Myers, William. ed. 2007. *The Origianal African Heritage Study Bible.* Valley Forge: Judson Press.

Paine, John. 2013 https://sharedveracity.net/2013/04/ (Accessed September 2, 2019)
Thurman, Howard. 1949. *Jesus and the Disinherited.* Nashville: Abingdon Press.

Townes, Emilie M. 2011. "Ethics as an Art of Doing the Work Our Souls Must Have." *In Womanist Ethics: A Reader*, edited by Katie Geneva Cannon, Emilie M. Townes, and Angela D. Sims, 35-50. Louisville: Westminster John Knox Press.